MAKE A DIFFERENCE

Following Your Passion
and Finding Your
Place to Serve

JAMES A. HARNISH

Abingdon Press / Nashville

MAKE A DIFFERENCE
FOLLOWING YOUR PASSION AND FINDING YOUR PLACE TO SERVE

This book is printed on elemental chlorine-free paper.
Library of Congress Cataloging-in-Publication Data hsa been requested.
ISBN 978-1-5018-47585

17 18 19 20 21 22 23 24 25 26 — 10 9 8 7 6 5 4 3 2 1
MANUFACTURED IN THE UNITED STATES OF AMERICA

In memory of my parents
who made a profound difference
in the lives of their children and inspired us to _
make a difference in the world.

You've taught me since my youth, God,
and I'm still proclaiming your wondrous deeds!
So, even in my old age with gray hair,
don't abandon me, God!
Not until I tell generations about your mighty arm,
tell all who are yet to come about your strength,
and about your ultimate righteousness, God,
because you've done awesome things!

(Psalm 71:17-19)

CONTENTS

ABOUT THE AUTHOR
& VIDEO PANEL

The Author

JAMES A. HARNISH is the author of numerous books and Bible studies, including *A Disciple's Path, A Disciple's Heart, Strength for the Broken Places, Earn. Save. Give.,* and *You Only Have to Die.* He is an acclaimed pastor and ordained elder in The United Methodist Church who has led congregations throughout Florida, most recently Hyde Park in Tampa where he served for twenty-two years. He lives in Winter Haven, Florida, with his wife, Martha, and enjoys writing, reading, and playing with his grandchildren.

The Video Panel

NICK CUNNINGHAM is the pastor of discipleship at Mt. Horeb United Methodist Church in Lexington, South Carolina. He previously served as the executive pastor of Teaching at Ginghamsburg Church in Tipp City, Ohio. Nick is a gifted communicator and strategist who loves to craft discipleship cultures that encourage followers of Jesus to embrace the full life of God. He is the author of *One: A Small Group Journey Toward Life-Changing Community* and *Forward: A Small*

Group Journey Toward a Full Life in Christ. Nick and his wife, Lindsey, have three children.

LINDSEY KRINKS is cofounder of Open Table Nashville, an interfaith homeless outreach nonprofit. She currently serves as the education and street chaplaincy coordinator and has deep roots in the homeless outreach and organizing communities. For the last ten years, Lindsey has worked on the underside of Nashville—the streets, encampments, jails, slums, and underpasses—while also working with faith leaders, community organizers, and public officials to make the city a more hospitable and just community. On any given day, she can be found in tent cities, washing feet on the streets, leading groups around downtown, marching for social and economic change, and foraging for native herbs and plants.

DJ DEL ROSARIO is lead pastor of Bothell United Methodist Church, a multisite congregation in Bothell, Washington. An ordained elder in the Pacific Northwest Annual Conference, DJ has served previously as associate pastor at Faith United Methodist Church and pastor of Lynden Faith United Methodist Church. He has also served as the director of young adult ministries, discernment, and enlistment at the General Board of Higher Education and Ministry, and as the executive director of Spark12.org. He is the author of *Wind in the Wilderness: A Lenten Study from the Prophets* and served on the advisory team for the United Methodist Confirmation curriculum. DJ and his wife have three daughters.

LISA YEBUAH is an ordained elder in the North Carolina Annual Conference. She currently serves as the pastor of the Southeast Raleigh Table, the third campus of Edenton Street United Methodist Church, located in downtown Raleigh. Lisa finds joy speaking throughout the United Methodist connection and seeks to inspire others to engage in parish-driven ministry. She loves CrossFit, spending time with friends, and binge watching episodes of *The Office*.

INTRODUCTION

Tell me, what is it you plan to do
with your one wild and precious life?
Mary Oliver[1]

This question has haunted me since I first came across it in the poetry of Mary Oliver. It's the persistent question that tugs on our hearts when we see the brokenness, injustice, violence, and pain of our world. It's the question that entices our imaginations when we catch a glimpse of how good life can be when ordinary people find their way to participate in God's extraordinary work of transformation in our world. It's the question that touches the deep desire of every follower of Christ to make a difference in this world. How would you answer it?

Across more than four decades of pastoral ministry, I've been fascinated by the way different people in unique and varied ways have found their own answer to Oliver's question, even if they have never heard of the poet. Admiral Joe Fowler was one of those people. He was ready to turn one hundred when he died. Even now I still hear the sound of his laughter, feel the strength of his handshake, and remember the passion with which he lived.

Born in 1894, Joe graduated second in his class at the US Naval Academy in 1917. After serving in World War I, he earned a degree in naval architecture from Massachusetts Institute of Technology in 1921. He designed and supervised the building of the world's largest aircraft carriers and supervised the West Coast shipyards during World War II.

Joe had already passed his sixtieth birthday when Walt Disney hired him to supervise the construction of Disneyland in California. When Disney complained to Joe about the cost of the construction, Joe told him that it cost a lot because he was building it to last a long time. When Disney began to dream of what would become Walt Disney World in Florida, he turned the planning and construction over to Joe. He retired at the age of eighty-four, but returned as a consultant during the construction of Disney World in Japan. Across his career, his typical response to every challenge was a cheerful, "Can do! Can do!"

Joe had passed ninety when I became his pastor, but I was captivated by his endless curiosity, boundless energy, and exuberant laughter. One day I asked, "What is the secret of your longevity and joy?" Without hesitation, he declared in no uncertain terms, "I wake up every morning asking myself what I can do to help my fellow man today!"

It was Joe's way of describing his passion to make a difference. Across his long life, his energy was constantly renewed by his desire to help someone else and make the world a better place.

You and I may never design aircraft carriers or build another Disney World, but we are all a lot like Joe Fowler. In our own unique way, we all ask the questions: *What can I do that will make the world a better place today? How can I make a difference?*

The questions take on a unique urgency for every follower of Jesus Christ:

- How can my life, talents, energy, and relationships become a part of the answer to our prayer that God's kingdom will come and God's will be done on earth as it is in heaven?

- How can I participate in God's work of healing, justice, peace, and reconciliation in this world?
- How can the love of God that became flesh in Jesus become a flesh-and-blood reality through me?

As we answer those questions, we not only experience transformation in our own lives but we also fulfill our mission as United Methodists: "to make disciples of Jesus Christ *for the transformation of the world.*"[2] It's our present-day version of John Wesley's conviction that "the world is [our] parish." We become disciples not for our own sake and not for the sake of sustaining a religious institution, but for the sake of God's transforming work in the world. We are "saved" in order to participate in God's salvation of others and God's redemption of the whole creation.

The good news is that the God who created you wants your life to make a difference even more than you do! The voice within us that challenges us to make a difference is none other than the voice of God. It is a part of the *imago dei*, the image of God, implanted deep within our souls. It's the voice of the God who spoke through Isaiah:

> *But now, says the LORD—*
> *the one who created you, Jacob,*
> *the one who formed you, Israel:*
> *Don't fear, for I have redeemed you;*
> *I have called you by name; you are mine.*
> *(Isaiah 43:1)*

From Genesis to Revelation, the Bible is the surprising story of the way God invites ordinary people—like Abraham and Sarah, Esther and Abigail, David and Jonah; fishermen like Peter and Andrew, James and John; women like Mary Magdalene and Lydia—to participate in God's extraordinary work in this world. Accomplishing God's purpose through people like every one of us is evidently God's idea of a good time! Roman Catholic priest and popular author Richard Rohr says, "God seems to want *us* to be in on the deal! The Great Work is ours too."[3]

God's passionate desire is for our lives to make their own unique contributions to the healing of a broken world. Our desire to make a difference is a finite expression of the infinite compassion of God who caught Moses' attention through a burning bush and said: "I've clearly seen my people oppressed in Egypt. I've heard their cry of injustice because of their slave masters. I know about their pain. I've come down to rescue them....So get going. I'm sending you to Pharaoh to bring my people, the Israelites, out of Egypt" (Exodus 3:7-10).

In one of Jesus' best-known parables, that same divine compassion moved with a visceral urgency in the heart of a nameless Samaritan so that he took action when we saw a naked, bloody man on the side of the road. He bandaged the man's wounds, placed him on his own donkey, took him to the inn, and promised to pay the bill. In that same compassion, Jesus continues to challenge his followers, "Go and do likewise" (Luke 10:37).

One of the sure signs of our continued growth as followers of Christ is that we feel our hearts being broken by the things that break the heart of God. Growing into the likeness of Christ means being drawn more deeply into the compassion of God so that we hear the cries of injustice in our world, see the broken people along the way, and seek with a divine urgency a way to make a difference in places of suffering, injustice, and pain.

It's also good news that we are not called to do this alone. Being "born again" means that we are born into the family of God with brothers and sisters in Christ, who share the same vision, burn with the same passion, and live by the same hope. Paul said that our unique talents, passions, and personalities are gifts of God's grace that are drawn together in the body of Christ to accomplish God's purpose in this world (1 Corinthians 12:1-12). We do not do this work alone; we do it together.

The best part is that we do not depend on our own wisdom, strength, or power. The same God who calls us to the task promises to provide the power to accomplish it (Philippians 1:6). We have access to "the overwhelming greatness of God's power that is working among us believers....the energy of God's powerful strength" (Ephesians 1:19). Paul is clear that "we have this treasure in clay pots so that the awesome power belongs to God and doesn't come from us" (2 Corinthians 4:7).

The purpose of this resource is to help you find the way you can make a transformative, Kingdom-shaped difference in this world as a disciple of Jesus Christ. It grows out of the essential practices of discipleship and is rooted in a deeply Wesleyan understanding of Scripture and spiritual formation.[4] You will be encouraged to do this by personal reflection on Scripture and shared discovery in a small group of fellow disciples. This book serves as the basic resource, along with the leader guide and video conversations with a diverse group of pastors who share their insights and invite you into the conversation. Each week, we will explore one of the basic steps along the way by finding examples in the real stories of ordinary men and women who have found their way to make a difference.

I'm grateful for the network of lay and clergy disciples who have participated with me in this project by responding to a preliminary survey and sharing their own insights and experiences. Our conversations have helped shape every part of this resource. We invite you into the conversation with us and with a small group of disciples who share the journey with you.

Martin Luther, the leader of the Protestant Reformation in the sixteenth century, left behind the records of his "Table Talk." These were conversations around the dinner table in Luther's home or notes taken during walks in his garden or on his travels. In a similar way, the spiritual awakening that gave birth to the Methodist revival in eighteenth-century England began with a small group of students at Oxford University who became known as "the holy club" because of the methodical way they shared their lives in intimate conversation, held each other accountable for their discipleship, and demonstrated their commitment to Christ by their engagement with the needs of the community around them. Wesley developed that pattern of "holy conversation" into the network of small groups that became the place where genuine transformation happened in people's lives and which continue to be a critical component of our life today. In the tradition of both Luther and Wesley, each chapter includes "Table Talk" with the members of our pastoral video panel and invites you to join our conversation. It's also our encouragement for you to participate in this study in a small group of disciples who are following their passion and finding their way to serve along with you.

One of my most rewarding experiences in pastoral ministry has been sharing the excitement, challenge, and sheer joy that faithful people experience when they realize that God can use their unique talents, opportunities, and strengths as a part of God's transformation in the lives of other people and in the world around them. I've seen the difference it makes in their lives when they follow their passion and find their place to serve. I look forward to sharing some of their stories with you and pray that the Spirit of God will use this time together to make a joy-filled, Kingdom-shaped, Christlike difference in your life so that you can make a difference in this world!

Chapter 1

AWAKENING!

What is important is anyone's coming awake.... What is important is the moment of opening a life and feeling it touch—with an electric hiss and cry—this speckled mineral sphere, our present world.

—Annie Dillard[1]

The fact that you opened this book means that you want your life to make a difference. What awakened that desire in you? Perhaps you sensed something (or Someone) tugging on your heart when you became painfully aware of some of the deep needs in your own life, in the lives of people you love, and in the needs of the often-confused and conflicted world around you. Perhaps you felt an inescapable longing to be and do more in the future than you have been or done in the past. You might be wrestling with a divine dissatisfaction with the way the world is and feel a relentless desire to do your part to make it a better place. It may be that in prayer, in worship, or in a small group with other followers of Christ, you've heard a word that took you by surprise because it was unmistakably God's word for you.

You may have noticed that people who make a Christ-centered difference in this world are often like the central characters in the movie classic *The Blues Brothers*. They are motivated by a deep, inner conviction that they are on a mission from God. Along the journey of discipleship, they heard and continue to hear what faithful people in every generation have identified as a "call" from God. In sometimes subtle and often surprising ways, they have come awake to some task that is greater than their own self-interest and beyond their own ability to fulfill. Their lives are open to a significantly larger, frequently more complex, and sometimes deeply disturbing world. They are often excited, perhaps confused, and ceaselessly energized by the possibility that their one wild and precious life can make a difference.

As you follow your passion and search for your place to serve, you will also discover that awakening to God's call is not a one-time experience but an ongoing process by which the Spirit of God continues to open our eyes to new ways of serving as we grow in our discipleship, as we face major transitions in our lives, and as we become more fully awake to the constantly changing needs of the world around us. The process is another step along the spiritual journey that John Wesley called "Christian perfection." It's the lifelong process by which the Spirit of God shapes our lives into the likeness of Christ. It leads us more deeply into the love of God and guides us to new opportunities to love others the way we have been loved by God.

Our primary calling to be faithful disciples who make a transformative difference in the world never changes. Jesus' initial call to every disciple is "Come, follow me" (Matthew 4:19). But the way we live out that calling will change in significant ways throughout our lifetime. It will take different forms as we begin to see this world and the people in it through the lens of God's extravagant love and grace revealed in Jesus. It will expand as we catch a glimpse of God's vision of reconciliation and healing for the whole creation. It will continue to be the unique way in which the Spirit of God awakens us to this life-transforming reality: God calls ordinary men and women like every one of us to be the people through whom God's kingdom comes and God's will gets done on this earth, even as it is already fulfilled in heaven.

I don't know Who—or what—put the question....But at some moment I did answer *Yes* to Someone—or Something—and from that hour I was certain that existence is meaningful and that, therefore my life, in self-surrender, had a goal. . . . I learned, step by step, word by word, that behind every saying in the Gospels stands *one* man and *one* man's experience.
—Dag Hammarskjöld (1905–61)[2]

As I look back across my own life, I can clearly identify times when I have been awakened to a new way in which God is calling me to serve. While my life as a disciple has been what Nietzsche called a "long obedience in the same direction,"[3] living in obedience to that call has led to major changes in the ways I've served and the needs to which I have responded.

Like the young Samuel (1 Samuel 3:1-11), I grew up in a home and church in which I was constantly encouraged to listen for and respond positively to Jesus' invitation, "Follow me." I began saying yes to that invitation in worship and Sunday school, at summer youth camps, and at an old-fashioned Methodist camp meeting. While I was in high school, I was awakened to the possibility that God was calling me into pastoral ministry. Over time, that calling became clearer and was confirmed in numerous ways. That calling has never changed. But in my first appointment, obeying that call meant investing myself in ministry with youth. Those young people are now adults who are passing on what I shared with them to their children and grandchildren. God called some of them into ordained ministry. Others have found their way of making a Christlike difference through their involvement in the church or through their careers and their engagement with the needs of the world around them. When I moved to a small, rural community, I learned how to be in ministry with fern and citrus growers.

When I was appointed to launch a new congregation in the rapidly growing suburbs of Orlando, obeying that call focused on finding ways to connect with people who had never been engaged with the church or people who had been burned by their experiences in it. Some people refer to these folks as the "nones" and the "dones." You may, in fact, be among them. This ministry demanded that I learn new skills, gain new understandings, and stretch my gifts in new ways. In later years, my gifts were poured into the reawakening of a century-old, urban-center congregation, a task that again required new ways of learning and serving.[4] The opportunities that came my way meant that I was constantly being challenged to change and grow in the way I obeyed God's call. As I prepared to retire, I prayed that the Spirit that had led me in the past would awaken me to new ways to live out my calling in the future.

That's my story, but you don't have to be a pastor to go through those kinds of changes. I've watched faithful laypersons find new ways to serve after they faced changes in their lives and as they grew in their faith. For example:

- I've seen married couples discover that their calling was radically different when they were young adult parents with dual careers raising small children, in contrast to the way they served when they became empty nesters and again when they retired.
- I've made the journey with men and women who awakened to God's call in the aftermath of a divorce, the loss of a career, a battle with cancer, or the death of a spouse.

- I've encouraged people who returned from a mission trip with a new passion to confront the systemic injustice and racism in their community.
- I've supported people who discovered that their years of experience in politics was precisely the gift that God could use to impact their city, state, or nation.
- I've joined people who were motivated to engage in public protests when they were awakened to the ways governmental policies were impacting poor or marginalized people.

Each person was awakened to new ways in which Jesus' call to discipleship was being lived out through them and to the new ways they could make a difference in this world.

New occasions teach new duties;
Time makes ancient good uncouth;
They must upward still, and onward,
who would keep abreast of Truth.
—James Russell Lowell (1819–91)[5]

John Dormois was one of those disciples who awoke to a new way to make a difference. He had a full career as a cardiologist, but as he grew in his faith and listened more deeply to the Spirit of God, he was awakened to the need for more effective end-of-life care. He saw the need for physicians to be responsive to the spiritual as well as the medical condition of their patients. At sixty-five years of age, he sensed a new calling from God. He closed his cardiology practice, laid aside his physician's name tag, and signed up for a semester in clinical pastoral education as a hospital chaplain. Following that experience, he went to Duke Divinity School where he earned a master of divinity degree with specific interest in their program on care at the end of life.

After graduation, he returned to Tampa where he serves as a palliative care physician with hospice and teaches both medical students and undergraduate premed students at the University of South Florida to be more effective in responding to the spiritual needs of their patients. He and his wife are also equipping people in their congregation to offer strength, compassion, and hope to people who are facing difficult end-of-life decisions.

Wherever you are along your journey of faith, the important thing is coming awake to the new task to which God is calling you in the present moment. It means listening for the same word that came to the prophet Isaiah: "Look! I'm doing a new thing; now it sprouts up; don't you recognize it?" (Isaiah 43:19).

A Wake-Up Call for Slumbering Saints

Here's the catch. It's frighteningly easy to fall asleep and miss out on the way God wants to use our lives to make a difference in this world. It happens when we are not fully awake to the voice of God's Spirit within us or the needs of the world around us.

Staying awake was an embarrassing challenge for one of our bishops during the opening session of the World Methodist Conference in Nairobi, Kenya. I watched him struggle to stay awake until he finally nodded off with his chin resting on his chest. Unfortunately, he was sitting directly behind the podium where everyone in the assembly could watch him. I sympathized with him when I learned that his flight had been delayed so that he arrived in Nairobi just in time to rush from the airport to the service—with no opportunity to adjust to a seven-hour time change. If you've made that kind of trip, you know that it can happen to any of us!

If you've ever fallen asleep in church, take heart! There's a biblical precedent for your sermonic slumber. In the Book of Acts, Luke tells the humorous story of a young disciple named Eutychus who "was sinking into a deep sleep as Paul talked on and on" (Acts 20:9). Long sermons tend to have that effect on a lot of people! Unfortunately, Eutychus was sitting in a third-floor window. In his sleep, he tumbled out of the window and down to the ground. Everyone assumed that he was dead. But "Paul went down, fell on him and embraced him, then said, 'Don't be alarmed. He's alive!'" (Acts 20:10). In the next verse, Luke records that Paul went back upstairs and kept preaching until daybreak.

Eutychus's story brings to mind Washington Irving's intriguing tale about Rip Van Winkle. The lazy, henpecked Dutch farmer went to sleep one day in the Catskill Mountains of New York after a mythical encounter with the ghosts of Henry Hudson's crew. He woke up twenty years later and found himself in a radically different world because he slept through the American Revolution. When he noticed that a picture of King George III over the tavern door had been replaced with a picture of George Washington, he declared himself a loyal subject of the king, unaware that a whole new government was now in charge.

The hard truth in Rip Van Winkle's story is that it can happen to any of us. It's a story about what happens when we are so intoxicated by memories of the past that we sleep through the revolutionary changes that are happening in the present. For people of faith, it can serve as a warning about how tempting it can be to drift into a drowsy spirituality so that we miss out on the new things God wants to do in and through our lives. It can happen to any of us when we become so comfortable with life the way it is that we miss out on what it can become.

The people of Israel had evidently drifted into somnambulant spiritual complacency while they were exiles in Babylon. They were aliens in a foreign land, living in a different culture under the authority of unfamiliar rulers. I'm sure they felt that they were powerless to make any difference in their circumstances. As a result, they must have been surprised when Isaiah announced a message from God that woke them out of their spiritual slumber.

> *Arise! Shine! Your light has come;*
> *the* L<small>ORD</small>*'s glory has shone upon you.*
> *Though darkness covers the earth*
> *and gloom the nations,*
> *the* L<small>ORD</small> *will shine upon you;*
> *God's glory will appear over you.*
>   *(Isaiah 60:1-2)*

Paul reached back to Isaiah's words when he challenged the disciples in Ephesus, *"Wake up, sleeper! Get up from the dead, and Christ will shine on you"* (Ephesians 5:14). It was his wake-up call for slumbering disciples in every place and time.

You'll find a similar wake-up call in the opening pages of the New Testament book of Revelation. John introduces himself to his readers as "your brother who shares with you in the hardship, kingdom, and endurance that we have in Jesus" (Revelation 1:9). John is one of us. He has shared the hardship, frustration, and weariness that every follower of Jesus sooner or later experiences. As a political exile on Patmos, he must have felt incapable of having any real impact on the expansive power of the Roman Empire. Like all of us, he must have wondered if there was any way he could make a difference. But he also knows the promise and hope of the kingdom of God, already present though not yet fulfilled among us.

John reports, "I was in the spirit on the Lord's day" (Revelation 1:10 NRSV). Some translations say John was "in prayer." The Common English Bible calls it "a Spirit-induced trance." I like to imagine that John fell asleep in church that day. Perhaps the sermon was so long that it had the same effect on John as Paul's marathon sermon did for Eutychus. In any case, John was surprised when he was suddenly awakened by "a loud voice that sounded like a trumpet" (Revelation 1:10).

There are 108 references to trumpets in the Common English Bible, fifteen of them in Revelation. Sometimes they invite people to gather for worship. Sometimes they are used to send troops into battle or to celebrate a victory. Sometimes they warn people of danger. In Revelation, trumpets announce John's apocalyptic visions of God's judgment. The one thing all the biblical trumpets have in common is that they arouse God's people and call them into action. Trumpets change the status quo; they disrupt the ordinary patterns of life; they demand a response. Trumpets energize people to get up and do something!

You may not have fallen asleep in church recently or been aroused by trumpets blaring, but your desire to make a Kingdom-shaped difference in this world means that the same Spirit that awakened John in Revelation has been awakening that passion in your life. This would be a good place to pause and ask a few intriguing questions.

- What's behind your desire to make a difference? Where did it come from?
- How have you felt or heard a call from God in your life?
- How have you been awakened to a new way of serving?
- What are you doing to stay awake to the Spirit's continuing call in your life?

The challenge for followers of Christ in every age is to listen for the sound of a trumpet that wakes us up to the new things God is doing in our world and energizes us to make a Kingdom-shaped difference in it. I'd like to suggest several practices that can help us stay awake to God's call.

Remember Who You Are

If we listen deeply, we will hear the voice of the Spirit saying, "Wake up! Remember who you are." Our calling is grounded in our identity as children of God. It is the word the Spirit speaks in baptism.

Luke records that when Jesus was baptized, "the Holy Spirit came down on him in bodily form like a dove." In a deeply personal way, the voice from heaven spoke directly to Jesus saying, "You are my Son, whom I dearly love; in you I find happiness" (Luke 3:21-22). The voice over the water declared that Jesus is the Son of God. He is as much of the infinite God as can be squeezed into finite, human flesh. It was an epiphany, a revealing of who Jesus really is.

Along with a declaration of who Jesus is, the voice over the water of baptism also declares who we are as followers of Jesus. In our baptism, the Spirit declares that we are sons and daughters of God. It's the epiphany that reveals what Richard Rohr calls "our deepest identity, our True Self, our unique blueprint."[6] That's who God says you really are!

I was reawakened to this truth by the arrival of our adopted grandchild.

Our daughter, Deborah, and our son-in-law, Dan, were at the hospital when Mattie, our adopted granddaughter, was born. We were in their home when they brought her from the hospital to welcome her into our family. Her birthday was a day none of us will ever forget. But along with her birthday, our daughter also celebrates what she calls "Gotcha Day." That was the day a few months later when the judge declared that Mattie is officially theirs and legally confirmed her name. Deborah celebrated the day on Facebook with this message:

> Happy Gotcha Day! This was the day the Judge declared that Mattie is stuck with us forever. No take backs. Love this girl like crazy. Can't wait to see who she becomes. God is good.

Every time United Methodists celebrate baptism, there is a place in the liturgy when the pastor turns to the congregation and says, "Remember your baptism and be thankful."[7] It's the invitation for every follower of Christ to once again hear the voice of God saying, "This is your Gotcha Day. You are my beloved son, my beloved daughter. No take backs. Love this child like crazy." As one of Jesus' disciples, your deepest identity is not primarily defined by the voices of the world around you but by the Spirit of God within you. It's the beginning of our call.

The painful truth, of course, is that we all too easily forget the voice of the Spirit and start believing other voices around us. We are constantly bombarded by a confusing cacophony of voices that try to convince us that our identity is defined by things like the model of car we drive, the label on the clothes we wear, the size of the check we can write, the place we were born, the political party we join, or the passport we carry. The voices around us try to brand us—and we often brand others—with labels that are more divisive than they are descriptive: conservative or liberal, black or white, immigrant or native, straight or gay, Republican or Democrat. The voices are loud and relentless. They keep trying to convince us who we are. Sometimes we start believing them. The experience is so universally true that you'll find it in surprising places.

I doubt that the Disney moviemakers had Christian baptism in mind when they produced *The Lion King*, but they told the same, primal story. The movie opens with a baptismal scene in which Simba, the lion cub, is lifted up as the son of the Lion King. But Simba runs away, forgets who he is, and starts living and acting as if he were less than the lion he was created to be. The story hinges on the moment Simba looks into the water where he sees his father's face and hears his father's voice. He tells Simba that he is more than he has become. The father's voice over the water tells Simba, "Remember who you are."

Jesus told his own version of this story. It's the story of a father who had two sons. One of the sons ran away from home, squandered his birthright, and ended up in the pigsty of his own selfishness. But Jesus said, "He came to himself" (Luke 15:17 NRSV). He remembered who he was. He remembered his "true self" and remembered the father who loved him. He picked himself up, turned around, and headed home. The biblical word for an act of turning like that is *repentance*. Jesus said that when the son was still a long way from home, his father saw him coming, ran to meet him, and welcomed him back into the life for which he was born (Luke 15:11-32).

The good news for every last, lost one of us is that when we forget who we are and fail to become all that God intends for us to be, the same God who claims us and calls us still declares, "You are my beloved son, my beloved daughter. Remember who you are."

A friend said he placed a small plaque at eye level beside the door the family always uses to go to school or to work. It simply says, "Remember your baptism." It was the daily reminder of who they are.

In the congregations that I served, we followed the liturgical year by celebrating "The Baptism of our Lord" on the first Sunday after Epiphany each year. At the climax of that service, we invited the congregation to come to the baptismal font, touch the water, and reaffirm the covenant with God that was made at their baptism. For people who had not been baptized, it was often the first step toward their commitment to Christ. Each year, I watched in amazement as the simple act of feeling the water flow through their fingers or placing it on their foreheads moved people deeply. I've never forgotten a man who turned from the font, stepped over to me, grabbed me by the arm, and said with tears, "I remember when you baptized me!"

I confess that I had forgotten. But that moment reminded me of the way he had turned away from the family's faith. He had never been baptized. He had gone through some very difficult times in his life. But he found a home in a church that affirmed the value of doubt and gave him the freedom to ask hard questions and search for his own answers. Along the way, he began to hear the voice of the Spirit inviting him for the first time to claim his identity as a child of God. With lots of questions still unanswered and a lifetime of searching ahead, he came for baptism and awakened to a new way of life. I had forgotten his baptism. But he had not forgotten, and neither did God. He has spent the years since that time discovering how his identity as a child of God is defining the way he is making a difference in the world.

Our calling begins at the waters of baptism where we hear the Spirit of God speak deeply into our own souls saying, "You are my son, my daughter." We can stay awake to God's calling by constantly remembering who we really are.

Reclaim Your Mission

The voice that sounds like a trumpet also says, "Wake up! Reclaim your mission."

Immediately following his account of Jesus' baptism, Luke records, "Jesus was about 30 years old when he began his ministry" (Luke 3:23). The baptism was not only God's confirmation of Jesus' identity; it was also God's commissioning of Jesus for his life of service. From there, Jesus was led into the wilderness where he wrestled with soul-level issues of his identity and his calling. He resisted the temptation to deny the identity his baptism had declared. From there he returned to his hometown in Nazareth where he announced his mission. It was not unlike the president giving the inauguration address that announces the agenda of the new administration. Jesus drew his mission from the prophecy of Isaiah:

> *The Spirit of the Lord is upon me,*
> *because the Lord has anointed me.*
> *He has sent me to preach good news to the poor,*
> *to proclaim release to the prisoners*
> *and recovery of sight to the blind,*
> *to liberate the oppressed,*
> *and to proclaim the year of the Lord's favor.*
> *(Luke 4:18-19)*

It was Jesus' self-declaration of his understanding of the mission to which God was calling him and the difference his life would make.

Again, our journey is patterned after Jesus' life. Being a follower of Christ means confronting our own temptations in the wilderness. There are times when our identity as children of God is tested; times when we are tempted to turn away from the call God has placed on our lives; times when we are tempted to try to accomplish God's self-giving purpose in our own, self-serving way. Like Jesus in the wilderness, we wrestle with deep questions about what it will mean for us to live in ways that are consistent with our identity as sons and daughters of God. And like Jesus, when we emerge from that wilderness place, we will have found a deep, inner clarity about who we are and why we are here. We go into the world with a powerful awareness of God's calling for us.

A few chapters later, we see that Jesus sent his disciples out with their mission, "to proclaim God's kingdom and to heal the sick" (Luke 9:2). They went with the audacious announcement, "God's kingdom has come upon you" (Luke 10:9). Luke also tells us that after the Resurrection, Jesus spent forty days with his disciples, "speaking to them about God's kingdom." He promised that the Holy Spirit would empower them to be his witnesses throughout the world (Acts 1:3, 8). At the center of Jesus' mission, and our own, is Jesus' vision of the Kingdom—the redemptive rule and healing reign—of God present though not yet fully realized among us.

Like Jesus' first disciples, we are sent into the world to be the agents of God's kingdom being realized in human history. That calling forces important questions upon us:

- What does the phrase "kingdom of God" mean to you?
- What would it look like for you to participate in that mission?

One of the ways we are continually awakened by God's Spirit is by reclaiming our mission as disciples of Jesus who are sent to be the living expression of the kingdom of God. But again, we soon discover how easy it is to lose sight of that mission. Like rocking ourselves to sleep in a rocking chair on the front porch on a sunny summer afternoon, we can easily rock ourselves into a subtle form of spiritual amnesia. Or like sleepwalkers who look like they are awake and alert but are actually wandering through life with no clear sense of where they are going, what they are doing, or why they are doing it, we lose sight of the direction in which we are going. We can become so preoccupied with unimportant things that we drift off into complacent irrelevancy. We can become so comfortable being inside the church that we forget that the church exists primarily for people who are outside of it. We forget that our mission is not to escape from the world but to participate in God's transformation of it.

The Church is in the world to save the world. It is a tool of God for that purpose; not a comfortable religious club in fine historical premises.
—Evelyn Underhill (1875–1941)[8]

At the organizing Conference of The Methodist Episcopal Church in America in 1784, our forbears declared that their mission was "to reform the continent and to spread scriptural holiness through these lands."[9] It was the soul-stirring mission that energized their passion and gave direction to their serving. It sent circuit riders across the American frontier establishing Methodist congregations and confronting the needs of the emerging nation. Continuing in that tradition, the current United Methodist mission declares that we are here to "transform the world." The point is that being a disciple is not simply about my life being shaped into the image of Christ; it is about the way God can use my life as a living witness to the kingdom of God, present though not yet fulfilled among us.

Clarity about how we individually participate in that mission often comes to us through other disciples. Rip Van Winkle's awakening came through an old woman who, "tottering out from among the crowd, put her hand to her brow, and peering under it in his face for a moment, exclaimed, 'Sure enough! it is Rip Van Winkle—it is himself! Welcome home again, old neighbor—Why, where have you been these twenty long years?'"[10] In the same way, the Holy Spirit often uses other disciples to help us find clarity in both our identity and our mission.

It happened for a friend in a Disciple Bible Study group. He had retired from a successful business career and was wondering how God might use him to make a difference in this new phase of his life. He was searching for his mission. He had no gift for teaching Sunday school, he couldn't sing in the choir, and he wasn't interested in serving on a committee, all of which are often the first things church folks think they are supposed to do. None of those ways of serving matched his personality, experience, or passion. Across the weeks of study, discussion, and sharing, the members of his group helped clarify his calling. He began using the same talents he had used in his career to establish and manage our congregational bookstore with the commitment that its resources would help other people grow in their discipleship and the proceeds would support mission partnerships beyond our local church. Because he followed his passion and found his unique place to serve, the bookstore now provides resources for growing disciples and makes major contributions to the church's mission partners every year. Through it all, he is experiencing exuberant joy in his ministry. He is grateful for the way his fellow disciples helped him reclaim his mission.

Renew Your Vision

We can also stay awakened to God's call when we listen for the voice that sounds like a trumpet saying, "Wake up! Renew your vision."

The Old Testament proverb reminds us, "Where there is no vision, the people perish" (Proverbs 29:18 KJV). Isaiah challenged the people in exile to keep their eyes open to the new things God was already doing among them (Isaiah 43:1). It's the continuing challenge to keep our eyes open for the new things God is doing in the world and wants to do through our lives. The Spirit calls us to watch for the way our life fits in to God's big vision of the healing of broken lives and the redemption of a broken creation. Looking back on his life and ministry, Paul told King Agrippa, "So, King Agrippa, I wasn't disobedient to that heavenly vision" (Acts 26:19). It's what people marching in the civil rights movement meant when they said and sang, "Keep your eyes on the prize and your hand on the plow."

In our daughter's "Gotcha Day" announcement for Mattie, she wrote, "Can't wait to see who she becomes." She's not the only one! Mattie's cousin, Julia, asked her mother, "Will Mattie grow up to look like Aunt Deborah and Uncle Dan?" That's a good question because our adopted grandchild's birth parents are African American; Mattie is black. Julia's mother wisely replied, "She won't look like them, but as she lives with them she will become like them in other ways." The Epistle of First John acknowledges the same truth about every one of us.

We have no idea what Jesus actually looked like, though we can be sure he looked more like a first-century Palestinian Jew than the long-haired, white, Anglo-Saxon Protestant many of us remember from typical depictions in art. But we know that when the Epistle of First John says that "we will be like him" (1 John 3:2), it has nothing to do with physical appearance.

It means that as we listen to Jesus' words, practice his teaching, grasp his vision of the Kingdom, absorb his spirit, and follow him in the way of servanthood that leads to the cross, the Holy Spirit will be at work within us to shape into his likeness in other, more formative ways. As we grow into the likeness of Christ, we will discover the love of God that became flesh in Jesus becoming flesh in us. As we live into his description of the kingdom of God, we become the answer to the prayer that God's kingdom will come and God's will will be done on earth, in and through our lives. As we look toward the promise of the fulfillment of God's vision for this creation, we find strength to live now in ways that are consistent with the way the world will be when God's saving purpose has been fully accomplished.

When I think about how easily we drift into spiritual slumber and lose sight of God's vision for us and for our world, I often remember Elizabeth Barrett Browning's words:

> Earth's crammed with heaven,
> And every common bush afire with God;
> But only he who sees takes off his shoes,
> The rest sit round it and pluck blackberries. [11]

So, how do we keep our eyes on the prize? How do we continually renew our awareness of the promise of God's kingdom coming among us? How do we remain awake to catch a glimpse of that Kingdom vision already present with us?

1. We can dig deeply into the prophetic visions in Scripture.

A fellow pastor who has spent a considerable amount of time among the Methodists in Cuba observed that Cuban preachers who are still serving under oppression often turn to the Old Testament prophets and the Book of Revelation for inspiration. That's not unusual. It's often been true of faithful people living under oppressive rulers throughout history. That is, in fact, where many of the biblical visions emerged.

God's vision of the future came to the prophetic author of Isaiah 40–66 when the covenant people were refugees in a foreign country under the ruling power of Babylon. Paul wrote some of his epistles while he was imprisoned in Rome. John received his revelation while he was a political prisoner on Patmos and the early church was suffering under the oppressive authority of the Roman Empire. Black slaves in the American South kept the biblical vision alive across generations of oppression by putting it into song. As we immerse ourselves in the prophetic words of Scripture, we can be reawaked to God's vision for the future.

2. We can keep company with faithful witnesses who have pointed the way to the fulfillment of God's kingdom through their lives and leadership.

Journalist William Allen White never forgot the day he met Theodore Roosevelt in the summer of 1897. White recalled, "He sounded in my heart the first trumpet call of the new time that was to be…the passing of the old into the new."[12] In the same way, we can be inspired by men and women who have awakened us to the vision of God's kingdom; faithful disciples who have demonstrated the passing of old ways of living and pointed us in the direction of the new life to which God is calling us.

In the eleventh chapter of the Letter to the Hebrews, the writer reminds the early Christians of the heroic men and women who went before them in the way of faithful witness and service. The memory of their lives is the basis for the challenge to "run the race that is laid out in front of us, since we have such a great cloud of witnesses surrounding us" (Hebrews 12:1). By keeping company with witnesses from the past, we are strengthened for our witness in the present. In that spirit, here are some of the faithful witnesses whose lives keep the vision alive in my life.

- Dietrich Bonhoeffer demonstrated the meaning of discipleship in his Christ-centered resistance to Hitler's power in Nazi Germany.
- Dorothy Day taught us to see God's kingdom at work in confronting economic and social injustice.
- Martin Luther King Jr. gave us the model of biblically rooted nonviolent change in opposing the racism in our nation.
- Mary McLeod Bethune broke through racial barriers by founding a school for African American girls that became Bethune-Cookman University.
- Nelson Mandela lifted the vision of liberation as a prisoner on Robben Island and showed us the way of reconciliation in his presidential leadership in South Africa.
- Jimmy Carter revealed the way of peacemaking in his presidency and modeled Christlike servanthood in his work with Habitat for Humanity.
- Pope Francis reveals the kingdom of God through his humility.

We can find strength for our journey by keeping company with those who have lived the vision before us.

3. We can keep our eyes open for ordinary people who, in small and seemingly insignificant ways, demonstrate God's vision of the Kingdom in their life of servanthood.

Keep your eyes open for faithful servants of Christ who are like mustard seeds, which, Jesus said, are the smallest of all seeds but which can grow into a flourishing bush. Their presence among us is like yeast, folded into the dough until it affects the whole loaf. You will often find them in unexpected places where faithful people have found their own way to make a Kingdom-shaped difference. We will be telling some of their stories as we continue through this study.

4. We can keep the vision alive by sharing our doubts, fears, questions, and hopes in community with fellow servants who share God's vision and keep it alive in us.

For more than three decades I've been a part of a small group of fellow pastors who meet twice a year for a three-day retreat. It's become a laughter-soaked community of faithful friends in which we celebrate our victories, unmask our fears, name our hopes, renew our vision, and find strength for our witness. Every time we gather, some of us come with excitement and joy to share the way we've seen God's Spirit at work in our lives. At the same time, some of us will come carrying heavy burdens, feeling deep pain, wrestling with hard questions, and searching for a renewal of our hope. Regardless of what we bring, we always leave with renewed passion and reawakened vision because of the things we have shared together.

Keep Listening for the Trumpet Sound

The same Spirit that awakened John when he was asleep in worship spoke with the sound of a trumpet to the people in Sardis: "Wake up and strengthen whatever you have left, teetering on the brink of death, for I've found that your works are far from complete in the eyes of my God. So remember what you received and heard. Hold on to it and change your hearts and lives" (Revelation 3:2-3). It is the Spirit's persistent wake-up call for every slumbering saint. I hear the Spirit saying, "Don't give up! God isn't finished with you yet! Strengthen what you have left! Remember what you have received from your past and use it to energize you for the future." It's the sure sign that God is always doing some new thing and is always inviting us to become a part of it.

While working on this book, I consulted with a team of church leaders who are investing their energies with United Methodist congregations in declining communities that are not unlike the church in Sardis. Cultural change and economic decline indicate that the odds are very thin that these communities and congregations will ever see the return of the "glory days" of their past when the neighborhoods were expanding and their pews were full. But this team is sounding the trumpet to awaken these declining congregations to remember what they have received, to strengthen what they have left, and to discover the way they make a Christ-centered difference by offering a word of hope and healing in the lives of people in the communities around them.

The Spirit still comes with a voice that sounds like a trumpet: Wake up! Remember who you are! Reclaim your mission! Renew your vision! God always has some new way of making a difference in your life so that you can make a difference for others.

When Winston Churchill planned his funeral, he left instructions that the service would conclude with a common practice in the British military. A bugler in "Whispering Gallery" of St. Paul's Cathedral played "The Last Post" which signals the end of the day. It's like the American tradition of playing "Taps" at the end of the day or at a military burial. "The Last Post" was followed by two minutes of silence after which a trumpeter above the west entrance sounded "Reveille." The word literally means "wake up." It is the universal call to action.[13] It was like the trumpet call that awakened John on that Sunday morning on Patmos. It's the voice of the Spirit that awakens each of us to get up and make a Kingdom-shaped difference in our world.

The world doesn't need any more slumbering saints, but the world is desperately in need of ordinary people—like you—who hear the sound of a trumpet that awakens them to the challenge and opportunity of being a part of God's extraordinary work of transformation in this world. The desire you feel deep within your soul for your one wild and precious life to make a difference is nothing less that the voice of the Spirit of God calling you. What matters is staying awake!

Table Talk

Welcome to the table! On these pages, you'll find comments from our video panel—both on and off camera. Whether you join us alone or in a small group, we invite you to use them as a springboard for your own reflection and discussion.

JIM: Thinking about my own awakening, I remember serving as a ministerial intern in a low-income housing project in Pittsburgh where everyone was black. In the little town where I grew up, we never saw black people. Living in that neighborhood awakened me to a different world.

LISA: The faith community around me nudged me awake when I wanted to coast. They taught me that saying yes to Jesus isn't a passive thing. Folks saw things in me that I would have let lie dormant.

NICK: Awakening happens in places of disruption. You see the world for what it is, this beautiful place that's terribly broken. Commitment is birthed out of saying, "Whoa! Things aren't OK. How can I *not* do something about it?" Discipleship is being caught up in healing, restoring, and reconciling the world. I'm like, "Sign me up for that!"

DJ: My grandmother often told me, "When you were a baby, I prayed for you to become a pastor." She'd say, "I see this happening in you." She taught me to name where God is in other people's lives. Disruption is a great word to remind us we live in a world that feels dark but doesn't have to be.

LINDSEY: I relate to the word disruption, too. It wasn't until I started realizing how immense the hurt, trauma, and poverty were that I was disrupted. Someone said we're called to be

faithful, not comfortable. It's being willing to put ourselves into uncomfortable places and see how we grow in the tensions.

JIM: That's what happened when Moses heard God say, "I've seen the misery of my people." It was God's disruption in his life. How do we help others experience that disruption and wake up to God's call?

LISA: When something happens in the news, the question posed on a Sunday morning is, "What can I do?" People have moments of holy restlessness, a holy haunting that all is not right in the world. But God flips the script and says, "Moses, you go." I want to believe there's something in all of us that says, "I might be a part of the solution, by God's grace."

LINDSEY: Moses didn't feel like the right person to do it, right? There's a courage that has to awaken in people. That's what I've seen happening across the city in people saying, "Yes, I will do it."

DJ: I think we are initially drawn by urgency, "That's not OK!" If my kid is choking, I'm going to immediately reach out there and do something about it. I think that awakening begins by looking at the world and seeing what's not right.

It's your turn. How will you join the conversation?

Questions for Reflection

- When have you fallen asleep in church? In your spiritual life?
- How have you heard the voice of the Spirit in the past? How have you heard it more recently?
- Which Scripture reading in this chapter spoke most deeply to you? Why?
- How has the voice of the Spirit awakened your passion and led you into action?
- Who are the disciples in your life who can help to provide clarity about how you are to participate in God's kingdom mission?
- What is a next step you can take to find your place in God's continuing work of transformation in our world?

Prayer

I slip into sleep,
a deadness I seek,
a trance of avoidance,
distraction's pleasant coma.
I am numb to your world, O Christ,
to your suffering, your love,
unconscious of you here.

Awaken me.
Breathe yourself into me
and rouse me
from my fearful distance.
Let even pain keep me awake,
attentive to your pain

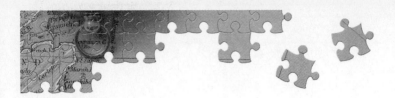

in all who hurt,
your love keep me alert
to love in all your forms.

Grant me this simple gift,
all you ask:
that I may stay awake,
trusting I am not orphaned,
and pray with you,
so earnestly praying for me
and all the world.
Just stay awake my little time
and pray with you.

Let all my waking hours
be wakeful hours.
—Steve Garnaas-Holmes[14]

Lord, awaken me and lead me into action so that I may participate in your
transformation of the world! Amen.

Action Ideas

- Remember your baptism and who you are in practical ways:
  - o Include the reminder of your baptism daily in your
    prayers, for example, "Most merciful and loving God, I
    have been baptized in your name, and I belong to you."
  - o Write the words of Luke 3:22; Romans 6:4; or Galatians
    3:26-27 (or another verse that proclaims who you are) on
    a notecard and post it where you will see it daily.
  - o Every time you shower or bathe or whenever it rains,
    allow the water to remind you that you are a baptized
    child of God.

- Renew your vision of God's kingdom mission by immersing yourself in the prophetic words of Scripture. (You might begin with Isaiah 40–66.)
- Be intentional in keeping company with other disciples and faithful witnesses as you participate fully in your small group or Bible study. Find an accountability partner, seek out a discipleship mentor, or volunteer to serve alongside others disciples.

Chapter 2

WHO ARE THESE PEOPLE?

I don't know what your destiny will be, but one thing I know: the only ones among you who will be really happy are those who have sought and found how to serve.

—*Albert Schweitzer (1874–1965)[1]*

Did Schweitzer get it right?

Did the theologian, musician, and physician who received the Nobel Peace Prize in 1952 for his medical mission in central Africa define the key to a happy life?

Are the only people who are really happy those who have found a way to serve?

If he got it right, how can you and I find that kind of happiness? What might that kind of life look like for us? Who are these happy people, anyway?

Look for Difference-Making People

As citizens of the United States, "the pursuit of happiness" is embedded in our cultural DNA. The Independence Day cover article of *Time* magazine pointed out in 2013 that while "all human beings may come equipped with the pursuit-of-happiness impulse...it's Americans who have codified the idea, written it into the Declaration of Independence and made it a central mandate of the national character."[2]

While happiness may be a "mandate of the national character," there is ample evidence in our contemporary culture that experiencing that happiness is becoming progressively more difficult for many people. In our type A, upwardly mobile, fast-paced, overachieving culture, the "pursuit of happiness" can easily be reduced to a manic attempt to work more, earn more, buy more, and achieve more in which the operative word is always *more*.

As a pastor, I've felt the frustration of people who, by the rest of the world's standards, have more than they could ever need but live with a nagging dissatisfaction in their souls. The things they've acquired and the success they've achieved have not made the difference they were hoping for. They are haunted by a desire for something more valuable and more lasting than anything money can buy. They still feel a gnawing desire for their life to make a more significant difference in the world.

Shame our wanton selfish gladness,
Rich in things and poor in soul.
—Harry Emerson Fosdick (1878-1969)[3]

I've prayed with people whose physical health has been compromised and counseled with people whose most intimate relationships have been shattered by the frantic pace at which they run after more of the things they already have. They experience about as much energy and passion as a bowl of wet noodles. All they've achieved and acquired hasn't satisfied the deep, inner longing for their one wild and precious life to make a transformative difference in this world. You may know people like that; you might be one of them.

But I've also known the kind of people Schweitzer described. They have found an unambiguous joy by discovering that their lives can make a difference. They are faithful disciples who have followed their passion, found their way to serve, and are making a real, tangible, transformative difference in the lives of others. They've seen small signs of the impact their witness is having on unjust systems and institutions. Seeing their lives, hearing their laughter, sharing their hopes, and listening to their stories confirm the truth in Schweitzer's words and the difference it makes for a person to find his or her custom-designed place to serve.

I've often discovered some of these people in likely places doing the kinds of things you might expect: teaching children in the Sunday school, serving in leadership in their congregation, singing in their church choirs and playing instruments in the worship band, facilitating small groups for spiritual growth, leading mission teams, visiting in hospitals and nursing homes, arranging flowers on the altar, or counting the Sunday offering.

I've also found these difference-making people in unlikely places doing things that you might not expect. I met them in homeless shelters and migrant farm worker camps. I found them delivering Meals on Wheels in economically underprivileged neighborhoods; registering voters in neglected communities; tutoring children in low-achieving public schools; organizing groups for economic justice; and creating bridges for communication between Christians, Muslims, and Jews. I stood with them in prayer vigils for nonviolence and saw them risk imprisonment because they refused to participate in war. I walked with them among the crowded tin shacks in the sprawling townships of South Africa. I've been humbled by their courageous witness for racial reconciliation. Wherever I found them, I also found a persistent passion and an incorrigible joy. *New York Times* columnist

David Brooks concluded that people like these "radiate a sort of moral joy." They possess "the self-effacing virtues of people who are inclined to be useful but don't need to prove anything to the world: humility, restraint, reticence, temperance, respect, and soft self-discipline."[4]

I've discovered that people who make a Kingdom-shaped difference often exude an inner peace that has a calming influence in places of conflict and stress. They face life with an amazing equilibrium and strength that provides stability to others in turbulent times. Their laughter comes from the same deep place as their tears and makes a joyful difference for the people they serve. Like the prophet Jeremiah, their passion is like a fire in their bones that nothing can put out (Jeremiah 20:9). It ignites a similar fire in others. They are like that enterprising woman in Proverbs 31 who "works with willing hands...girds herself with strength...reaches out her hands to the needy...and she laughs at the time to come" (Proverbs 31:13, 17, 20, 25 NRSV). They lead me to ask the same question that is asked of the white-robed saints in Revelation, "Who are these people...and where did they come from?" (Revelation 7:13). On a deeper level, I'm forced to ask how I can make the same kind of difference in the lives of others.

Lessons from the Farm

Becca Stevens is the kind of woman the writer of Proverbs celebrated and Schweitzer described. By following her passion and finding her place to serve, she is making a life-changing difference in the lives of women in her hometown of Nashville, Tennessee, and around the world. Becca was honored by CNN in 2016 as one of their "Heroes of the Year" because of her leadership in founding Magdalene, a residential community that brings healing and hope to women who have survived abuse, prostitution, human trafficking, poverty, and drug addiction. That ministry led to the establishment of Thistle Farms, a social enterprise that employs graduates of Magdalene in the production and distribution of natural body care items, scented candles, hand-made paper, and sewing items. They also operate the Thistle Stop Café in the heart of Nashville. In addition, Becca is an Episcopal priest who leads the campus ministry at Vanderbilt University, as well as an author and speaker on spiritual formation and social justice.

Becca's passion and calling grew out of her own experience of sexual abuse and her deep conviction that "Love Heals." When she was honored by CNN, she told the nation-wide television audience that she came to the stage barefoot as an expression of solidarity with women who are still walking the streets, searching for someone to lead them toward healing. She communicates the joy, humility, and self-discipline that David Brooks named as defining characteristics of people who make a transformative difference in our world.

When Margaret Went to Jail

Margaret Palmer is another woman who exudes the passion and joy that Schweitzer described because she has found her way to serve. Because of her obedience to God's call in her life, God has used her to make a Kingdom-shaped difference in the lives of both the women she serves and the volunteers who serve with her.

When I became her pastor, I found her to be an energetic, joyful, retired woman with a laugh that is just as real and deep as her faith. She made me smile every time she came through the door. But she seemed different the day she made an appointment to meet with me. I knew this would be a serious conversation, though I had no idea where it would lead.

I knew Margaret had been serving as a "Chat Lady" at the county jail. When I would ask her husband how Margaret was doing, he would reply with a smile, "She's in jail again."

The "Chat Ladies" began in a Bible study group in which Margaret and two other women realized that after years of studying the Scripture, it was time to do something with it. Having heard Jesus say, "I was in prison and you visited me" (Matthew 25:36) for the umpteenth time, Margaret felt an urgent calling to visit women in the county jail. She remembers how clearly God's call came to her and how terrified she was the first time she heard the iron gates at the jail lock behind her. Their only task was to be present with the women, to listen to their stories, and pray with them if they requested it.

Margaret says that women she previously would have thought very little of became "real people" to her. She no longer saw them as prisoners but as friends. She laughs with that effervescent joy when she says, "It was so much fun!"

But after ten years of weekly chats, Margaret became painfully aware that she was seeing some of the same women over and over again. She remembers how excited the women were when they were released. But they would go back to the same people engaging in the same drugs, alcohol, and petty crimes because they had nowhere else to go. Margaret was convinced that God had given her a vision of a home where recently released women would find security, support, and mentoring to begin a new life.

The need was obvious. Margaret's passion was unrelenting. But I didn't see how she could pull it off. She remembers that I was skeptical. I asked if there was any agency in the city that she might partner with on this, but she had already checked that out. No one was doing what needed to be done, and she was determined to do it. I suggested that she gather a few other people to pray with her about it.

As she left the office that day, I remembered Gamaliel, who said of the early Christians, "If their plan or activity is of human origin, it will end in ruin. If it originates with God, you won't be able to stop them. Instead, you would actually find yourselves fighting God!" (Acts 5:38-39). It turns out that I grossly underestimated both God's vision and Margret's passion.

In a short time, an amazing group of people caught Margaret's vision. An attorney provided pro bono legal assistance in setting up a 501(c)(3) nonprofit organization. A real estate agent led them to a home that was exactly what she had envisioned in a dream. The men's Bible study group in which her husband participated volunteered to do the renovations. They found the director for the ministry among women Margaret had met as a Chat Lady in the jail. In 2003 Hillsborough House of Hope welcomed its first residents.

Fifteen years after she shared her vision with me, the House of Hope is drawing support from across the city and providing the opportunity for a host of volunteers to find their place to serve. At ninety years of age, Margaret is still going strong. Rather than relax in her rocking chair, she now has a vision for another house where recently released women can live with their children. She is determined to keep on serving until they bury her ashes in the House of Hope flower garden, laughing all the way.

We cannot go into the salty waters made up of sweat and tears to love the world without being able to laugh....If anyone thinks that they can take it all in without laughing some of it off, they will drown in tears....The laughter and tears are both signs to me that it's time to cleanse, laugh, grow, and heal.
—Becca Stevens[5]

People like Becca and Margaret convince me that Schweitzer got it right. The people who are really happy and who make a Kingdom-shaped difference are those who have sought and found a way to serve. As I've listened to their stories, I've begun to see some common elements in their experience. Wherever their journeys take them, they generally begin at the same place.

Stay Connected to the Power Source

Richard Rohr, the Franciscan priest whose books have become a source of spiritual guidance to many, reported a Cape Town conversation in which Archbishop Desmond Tutu told him, "We are only the light bulbs, Richard, and our job is just to remain screwed in!"[6] It could have been the archbishop's paraphrase of Jesus' words, "I am the light of the world. Whoever follows me won't walk in darkness but will have the light of life" (John 8:12).

Margaret's passion for the House of Hope didn't drop in out of thin air. Becca's leadership of Thistle Farms doesn't function out of her own strength or goodness. In both cases, what they do is a result of who they are and of the way they remain connected to Christ. They demonstrate the practical necessity of Jesus' words, "Remain in me, and I will remain in you. A branch can't produce fruit by itself, but must remain in the vine. Likewise, you can't produce fruit unless you remain in me. I am the vine; you are the branches. If you remain in me and I in you, then you will produce much fruit" (John 15:4-6). Their unique ways of serving grew out of and are sustained by patterns of spiritual discipline including study of Scripture, Christian community, corporate worship, and a disciplined practice of prayer.

Becca's prayer life is ordered around the well-worn *Book of Common Prayer* that belonged to her father, an Episcopal priest who was killed by a drunk driver when she was five years old. She practices the centuries-old Order for Morning and Evening Prayer. At Thistle Farms, every day begins with the women gathered in a circle. They light a candle as a reminder of their calling to be a place that brings light into the darkness of broken lives. They share their joys and concerns and pray for God's Spirit to work through them that day.

Margaret's pattern of prayer includes daily quiet time reading Scripture and following a daily devotional guide. As her story revealed, she also engages in prayer with a small group that became the place where God first began to call her to her ministry. She simply bubbles over with laughter and a huge smile spreads across her face when she looks back across her life and says, "I'm no saint, but God and I have become very familiar."

People like Becca and Margaret know that they are not the light, but they become witnesses to the light of God's love in Christ because they stay connected to the source of power.

Listen for Your Name

At the Methodist camp meeting my family attended when I was a teenager, there was a chorus we sang over and over again until it was not only imbedded in our memory but also became a part of the pattern of how we lived:

> When He calls me I will answer;
> I'll be somewhere list'ning for my name.[7]

The song is based on the story of the way God's call came to a young boy named Samuel. In the background is the both miraculous and humorous story that led to the day Hannah brought her son to the old priest, Eli, saying, "I prayed for this boy, and the LORD gave me what I asked from him. So now I give this boy back to the LORD" (1 Samuel 1:27-28).

The young Samuel "served the Lord under Eli the priest" (1 Samuel 2:11). As the old priest's protégé, Samuel was learning his people's sacred words and stories and participating in the ancient disciplines of worship and prayer. All of these practices prepared him for what was to come. One night Eli, "whose eyes had grown so weak he was unable to see," was sound asleep while Samuel was lying down in the Temple, which means that he was close to the presence of God. Like John in the Revelation, he was awakened by a voice calling his name. Assuming it was Eli, he woke the old priest, who quickly told him to go back to sleep. After this happened three times, Eli realized that there was more going on here than a kid who was either having nightmares or was afraid of the dark. Eli told Samuel that if he heard the voice again, he should say, "Speak, Lord. Your servant is listening." That's what Samuel did. When the voice woke him again, Samuel responded, "Speak. Your servant is listening." That's when the Lord told him, "I am about to do something in Israel that will make the ears of all who hear it tingle!" (1 Samuel 3:1-11, esp. vv. 9, 11).

Here's the point: God's call usually comes to people who practice the spiritual disciplines that enable them to hear and respond to God's Spirit. They are consistent in their practice of worship. They soak themselves in the words of Scripture. They develop patterns of prayer that keep them awake and responsive to the new things God is doing and through which they discern the guidance of the Spirit. They live in community with other faithful disciples. Just the way Samuel was staying close to God's presence in worship and prayer, the people who make a God-centered difference practice the spiritual disciplines that keep them connected to the right power source. Samuel's story might also be a warning that listening for God's call might cause you to lose some sleep!

If I had one gift, and only one gift, to make to the
Christian Church, I would offer the gift of prayer.
For everything follows from prayer....Prayer is
not an optional subject in the curriculum of living....
It is the required subject.
—E. Stanley Jones (1884–1973)[8]

Throughout history, the people who make a world-changing difference in Jesus' name demonstrate the kind of spiritual discipline and listening prayer that Samuel's story conveys. In the stress of his struggle against Hitler, Dietrich Bonhoeffer underscored the importance of "daily, quiet attention to the Word of God" as the "focal point of everything which brings inward and outward order into my life."[9]

Bishop Rueben Job described the central role of prayer in the Methodist movement when he said that it is impossible to live the life of discipleship without the discipline of prayer. He wrote, "Our spiritual and even our physical lives become a shambles without the constant companionship with God that prayer alone can make possible." He caught the "methodical" discipline of the early Methodists in saying that "a life of prayer was not an accident…[but] the result of a determined and disciplined effort."[10]

John Wesley learned the importance of spiritual discipline by reading William Law's classic, *A Serious Call to a Devout and Holy Life*. Law was a quiet schoolmaster in Putney, England, whose writings inspired Wesley—along with William Wilberforce—and contributed to the religious revival in England and the Great Awakening in America. He also organized schools and homes for the poor and spoke out against the wars that had torn apart England in the aftermath of the Reformation.

John Wesley was a twenty-two-year-old student at Oxford when he read *A Serious Call*. He recorded in his journal, "The light flowed in so mightily upon my soul, that every thing appeared in a new view. I cried to God for help, and resolved not to prolong the time of obeying Him as I had never done before."[11] After reading Law's *Christian Perfection*, Wesley wrote that he "more explicitly resolved to be all devoted to God, in body, soul, and spirit."[12]

Wesley imbedded Law's emphasis on the necessity of spiritual discipline at the center of the early Methodist movement. In 1760, he wrote a letter of reproof and guidance to John Trembath, one of his early preachers who was evidently a gifted orator, but shallow in his spiritual discipline. Wesley's words to Trembath serve as a continuing challenge for all of us:

> O begin! Fix some part of every day for private exercises.... Whether you like it or no, read and pray daily. It is for your life; there is no other way, else you will be a trifler all your days.... Do justice to your own soul, give it time and means to grow. Do not starve yourself any longer.[13]

Your life of prayer may take many forms as you continue to grow. It will, in fact, need to be customized to fit your personality, experience, and lifestyle. In *A Disciple's Heart*, Justin LaRosa and I introduced *Lectio Divina*, Centering Prayer, and St. Ignatius's Prayer method as examples of the rich variety of patterns that can help you develop your own way of prayer.[14] The good news is that there is a wide range of resources available to assist you in developing your own personalized pattern of prayer. Whatever pattern you find to be most effective for you, the challenge from Mr. Wesley is always, "O begin!" The spiritual discipline of prayer that is grounded in Scripture and nurtured in worship is the starting point for our discovery of a life that really makes a difference. It is the sustaining center of a relationship with God that continues to fuel our passion and leads us to our place to serve. It is the renewing source of our vision for the future.

Hear and Respond

When we practice the essential spiritual disciplines, we are prepared to hear and respond to God's call whenever and wherever it may come. It happened for Albert Schweitzer "one brilliant summer morning" when he awoke to the realization that he could not accept his "good fortune as a matter of course, but must give something in return." He decided, "I would devote myself directly to serving humanity."

He wrote:

> I had already tried many times to find the meaning that lay hidden in the saying of Jesus: "Whosoever would save his life shall lose it, and whosoever shall lose his life for My sake and the Gospels shall save it." Now I had found the answer.[15]

It happened for Margaret as she practiced the spiritual disciplines of Scripture reading and prayer and listened to the stories of incarcerated women. It happened for Becca as she engaged with women who were surviving on the streets. Because God's calling is custom-designed for each of us, it might come in a different way for you. It came in a unique way for my friend, Rick.

I met Rick more than thirty years ago. He was a successful business-man with a day-brightening smile that could light up the room when he walked in. He started coming to church because he and his wife had a new son and he was feeling a sense of gratitude for the blessings in his life. He was also a first-class tennis player who attempted, with no success, to improve my game. As we became friends, we often laughed about some of the differences in our social and political convictions.

When I moved to a new pastoral appointment, I was grateful that he connected with my successor and continued attending worship with his family. Across the years that followed, I noticed a change in our conversations that gave evidence of his growing faith.

When the church began recruiting volunteers to serve in a public school in an underprivileged neighborhood, Rick told his wife, "I think Someone is telling me to do something." He contacted the principal and asked what they needed. Her immediate response was that they did not have funds to pay for the bus for the fourth grade students to go on the Florida history field trip. Rick immediately wrote the check to pay for the bus. He visited the school, got to know the teachers, and discovered that for many of the children, the free meal they received at school would be their only meal for the day. During Black History Month, Rick accepted the invitation to serve as a judge for the school speech contest. He was genuinely impressed by the speakers, one of whom went on to win the county championship. He arranged to celebrate math promotions by taking the students to a professional basketball game where they got to high-five the team on the court. As the years have gone by, he has continued to be engaged both financially and personally in the lives of those students.

There's no question that Rick is making a difference for the students. But when he describes the difference the experience has made in his life, that day-brightening smile spreads across his face. He laughs when he says that anything he has done for them is nothing compared to the difference they have made in his life. He has discovered the place where his great gladness and the world's great need meet.

The stories of these people and of others convince me that Schweitzer was correct. The people who are really happy are those who have sought and found their way to serve. They have learned to listen for the way the Spirit of God will speak to them because they practice the time-tested spiritual disciplines of the Christian life. They are ordinary people—just like us—who experience an extraordinary joy in knowing that their lives are making a Christlike difference in the lives of people around them and a Kingdom-shaped difference in the world. Because you're reading this book and sharing this study, my guess is that you want to make this kind of difference too!

Table Talk

Welcome to the table! Whether you join us alone or in a small group, we invite you to use these words from our video panel—both on and off camera—as a springboard for your own reflection and discussion.

JIM: Schweitzer said happy people are those who find their way to serve. How do we find our place to make a difference in people's lives?

LISA: A woman in our community has always loved horses. When she lost her job she located an organization that provides horse therapy with children. It was God's gentle way of calling her out of one thing into something she loved.

NICK: I resonate with this chapter and the importance of spiritual disciplines. Often we're only concerned with them when we're not sure what to do. Would we find ourselves in those places if we were attuning ourselves to God?

JIM: God can take the thing we love and use it to make a Christlike difference in somebody else's life.

LINDSEY: Anywhere we are, we're invited to jump in. We hold our possessions and plans so tight, but it isn't until we open our hands that we learn to live in this fully. It's fun! You cry and you laugh more deeply than you ever have.

LISA: Some individuals have to practice the practice of practice. They have to step out of their comfort zone and put themselves in a place God may be nudging them toward. They stumble into their calling.

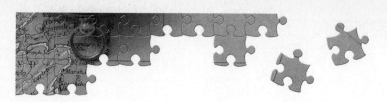

NICK: I think there's an innate desire in all of us to do good things. But we're also very inward. We have to be rewired, reprogrammed. Spiritual disciplines are super important.

LINDSEY: It's a willingness to give yourself to something bigger than yourself; being rooted in a bigger vision and knowing we're not going to see all the harvest. People who are rooted in that vision give themselves knowing that they're not going to do everything, but they're going to do a part of it.

JIM: That long vision is what keeps you going over the long haul. It's "a long obedience in the same direction."

DJ: Answering God's calling is often noticing where we are at this very moment—to really value and cherish where we are. How am I being a responsible steward in my context?

LINDSEY: I believe that wherever we are, God meets us there. Whether we're in an affluent church or on the streets, God meets us where we are.

LISA: I worked one summer with Alan Story in Johannesburg, South Africa. I was compelled by his deep love for Scripture. Alan really believed that the world could change. We hear, "This is just the way that it is." Alan believed, "No, actually we can bend toward God's resounding yes, and it can happen through the church." I'm grateful for folks who stand in the face of the noes and say *yes*.

It's your turn. How will you join the conversation?

Questions for Reflection

- What spiritual disciplines am I practicing that will prepare me to listen for and respond to God's call? What steps do I need to take to go deeper in them?
- How is the written word of Scripture becoming a living word in my life?
- How does the Christian community of which I am a part provide support, confirmation, and accountability for my calling?
- When I feel the nudge of God's Spirit, how do I respond to it?
- Am I experiencing the inner joy that comes to any follower of Christ who follows his or her passion and finds a place to serve? Am I demonstrating other characteristics common to those who are making a Kingdom-shaped difference (inner peace, strength, equilibrium/stability, passion)?

Prayer

Master, speak! thy servant heareth,
waiting for thy gracious word,
longing for thy voice that cheereth;
Master, let it now be heard.
I am list'ning, Lord, for thee;
What hast thou to say to me?

Speak to me by name, O Master,
let me know it is to me;
speak that I may follow faster
with a step more firm and free,
where the Shepherd leads the flock
in the shadow of the rock.

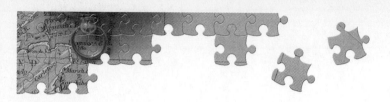

Master, speak, and make me ready
when thy voice is truly heard
with obedience glad and steady
still to follow ev'ry word.
I am list'ning, Lord, for thee:
Master, speak! O, speak to me![16]

Lord, open my ears so that I may hear your call and follow your leading!
Amen.

Action Ideas

- Incorporate one new spiritual discipline into your life, or give focused attention to a discipline that needs refreshing such as the study of Scripture, Christian community, prayer, or worship.
- Prioritize your participation in regular corporate worship.
- Develop a personalized pattern of prayer by experimenting with a variety of prayer methods. Search online and in books on prayer for descriptions of different prayer practices (e.g., *lectio divina*, the Ignatian method, praying the psalms, personalizing Scripture, the examen, the ACTS model, and many others).
- Choose a new-to-you prayer or devotional guide for the next thirty to forty days. If you have never used *The Book of Common Prayer* or a devotional guide based on it, this tool may help breathe new life into your prayer routine.
- Spend at least five minutes each day in focused listening prayer. Increase the time as you are ready and able. Try journaling what you hear and how you will respond.

Chapter 3

CHILDREN, GO WHERE I SEND YOU

The place God calls you to is the place where your deep gladness and the world's deep hunger meet.

—*Frederick Buechner[1]*

An African American spiritual says, "Children, go where I send Thee." It's a musical version of God's call to followers of Christ who are searching for the way they can make a difference in every generation. But Gert Rizzoli wasn't going anywhere. Her story is satire, but like every good satire, it has a ring of truth within it. The story imagines Gert sitting in the same place in the front row in her home church every Sunday morning. She loved being close to the pastor and having quick access to the restroom. Friends said she was a gracious, Christlike lady except when it came to giving up her seat. Gert was so faithful to her pew that when she died, her family installed a bronze statue of her on that front row, with her Bible open on her lap.

Gert's family was pleased, but other folks weren't so sure. A man who incurred Gert's wrath when he inadvertently took her spot described the statue as a frustrating reminder of that experience. He said, "It's like she's still there defending her seat." Another asked, "What if more people request the same thing? Pretty soon the church will be filled with bronze statues."[2]

This satirical story inspires humor, but I've known real people like the fictional Gert in every congregation I've served. Their faithfulness is defined by where they sit in worship, and God forbid that anyone else should take their seat! They are loyal to their church, committed to their discipline of worship, and intractable when it comes to being in their pew. That commitment should not be taken lightly. We need the witness of their faithfulness in a time when regular worship attendance is on the persistent decline.

In *A Disciple's Path*, Justin Larosa and I underscore the importance John Wesley placed on worship and the sacraments as essential spiritual disciplines for the early Methodists. It is inherent in our membership vows that include the commitment of "presence." Being a part of a worshipping congregation ignites our passion, nurtures our faith, unites us with other disciples, sustains our spirits, and empowers our witness. It is also the primary means by which the church proclaims the biblical word of justice and grace in the public arena. As we saw in the previous chapter, faithful participation in worship is a spiritual discipline that can awaken us to God's Spirit and prepare us to follow God's call. It's one of the ways God makes a difference in our lives that enables us to make a difference in the world.

So, let's lift a cheer for real people like the fictional Gert who bear witness to the difference it makes to live a life centered in the spiritual discipline of worship. But the satirical image of a bronze version of Gert, frozen in time on her favorite pew with her Bible in her lap, is a fundamental contradiction of an essential characteristic of our discipleship. Consider the following examples from Scripture:

- Jesus' invitation to the fishermen to follow him continued with his announcement that they would "fish for people" (Mark 1:17). They were not called to wait for people to come to them like fish jumping into their boat, but to go out in search of them.
- Jesus did not invite people to come into the synagogue to be healed; he sent his disciples into the communities around them to heal, teach, cast out demons, and announce the presence of the kingdom of God (Luke 9:1-5).
- At the Transfiguration, when Peter suggested that they camp out on the mountaintop of their spiritual experience, Mark graciously suggests that Peter didn't know what he was saying (Mark 9:6). They immediately came down from that spiritual high and were drawn into the needs of the messy, hurting, confused crowd that gathered at the foot of the mountain.
- At the Last Supper, Jesus offered a dramatic portrayal of servanthood by washing his disciples' feet and then said, "I have given you an example: Just as I have done, you also must do" (John 13:15).
- The angelic command at the empty tomb was not "Stay here and worship" but "Go, tell his disciples...that he is going ahead of you into Galilee. You will see him there" (Mark 16: 1-7, esp. v. 7).
- Jesus' final commission to his disciples was not "Come and sit in your pew" but "Go and make disciples of all nations, baptizing them in the name of the Father and of the Son and of the Holy Spirit" (Matthew 28:19).
- At the Ascension, Christ's last promise to his disciples was that they would receive power from the Holy Spirit to become his witnesses throughout the world (Acts 1:8).

In that spirit, the mission of The United Methodist Church announces that we do not "make disciples" for the sake of the church or for the sake of our own spiritual well-being, but *"for the transformation of the world."*

The practical implication of a biblical understanding of discipleship is that the Christian life is not primarily defined by sitting in the pew on Sunday morning but by the way we live and serve beyond the church walls during the week. We live out our discipleship in the world rather than inside the church. Our experience in worship is like the team gathering in the locker room before going onto the field where the real game will be played. What we do inside the church is intended to equip us to be the agents of God's love, grace, justice, and peace on the outside. Paul said that we are reconciled to God in Christ so that we can become the agents of God's reconciliation of the world (2 Corinthians 5:19).

The church is the presence of God in the world.
Really in the world, really the presence of God....
The church is the invasion of the world by miracle,
by the presence of the life-giving
God who calls [us] from death into life.
—Dietrich Bonhoeffer (1906–45)[3]

A pastoral colleague described this truth by building a sermon around the difference between spinning on a stationary bicycle and biking on the open road. Both provide exercise, but one of them doesn't get you anywhere. That's why it's called "spinning." It's done in an air-conditioned gym where we are protected from the risk of traffic or bad weather. Biking gets us out into the open, where we confront the challenge of whatever the natural elements throw at us. It takes us somewhere. With that metaphor, she drew the contrast between followers of Christ who are "spinning their wheels" inside the church and those who are living their faith by making a real difference in the risks, challenges, and opportunities that confront us in the world.

In his Letter to the Corinthians, Paul linked God's work in Christ with our service in the world when he wrote, "All of these new things are from God, who reconciled us to himself through Christ and who gave us the ministry of reconciliation" (2 Corinthians 5:18). The Incarnation means not only that God came among us in Jesus but also that God intends to go into the world in the lives of people like every one of us.

Living into these biblical texts, The United Methodist *Book of Discipline* declares that we make a Kingdom-shaped difference when we "send persons into the world to live lovingly and justly as servants of Christ by healing the sick, feeding the hungry, caring for the stranger, freeing the oppressed, being and becoming a compassionate, caring presence, and working to develop social structures that are consistent with the gospel."[4] To put it simply, we are called to *go*, following Jesus into the world.

A stained glass window in the Laurie Ray Memorial Chapel at Hyde Park United Methodist Church contains an image of Jesus with his hands outstretched, below which are the words "Come unto me." Today it is above the chancel, offering an open invitation to all who come to receive the bread and cup or those who kneel at the altar for prayer.

But when the chapel was originally built, the congregation faced the opposite direction. The stained glass window was above the doors that opened directly onto the sidewalk along a busy street that leads into downtown Tampa. People saw that image of Christ and read his words as they stepped out into the rush and risk of the city. I often wondered if the original intent was to hear the risen Christ saying, "Come unto me. I've already gone before you into the city. That's where you will find me."[5]

Of course, both interpretations are correct. Jesus welcomes us into the place where we hear the word preached, are baptized into the body of Christ, receive the bread and cup, are bound together in Christian community, and find strength for the life of discipleship.

But the other way of seeing it is equally true. The risen Christ who promised the first disciples that they would find him in Galilee calls us out of the church and into the world. By the power of the Spirit, we are sent as the agents of his healing, forgiveness, justice, and peace in the community beyond the church walls. It's a visual expression of the way our experience in worship empowers us to make a transformative difference outside the walls of the church. We are sent from worship to become the people through whom God answers our prayer for God's kingdom to come and God's will be done in our world. When we see the injustice and suffering of the world and ask, "God, why don't you do something about this?" we will probably hear God asking us the same question. God is already out there, and we are challenged to join him in the Kingdom work of healing, peace, and redemption.

Our life of discipleship begins in the church but it is completed in the world. Charles Wesley called the Holy Spirit we experience in worship the "sacred energy"[6] that sends us into the places where we live and work the rest of the week. In the same upper room where the risen Christ "breathed on them and said, 'Receive the Holy Spirit,'" he also said, "As the Father sent me, so I am sending you" (John 20:21).

The question for us is the same question Dietrich Bonhoeffer asked as he courageously confronted the growing threat of Hitler's rise to power in Germany. He wrote that "the most urgent problem besetting our Church is this: How can we live the Christian life in the modern world?"[7]

You Are Called to Love

Jere Gault never expected to spend a significant part of his time in retirement with migrant farm workers and their families. He describes himself as "an American who believes in border protection, fiscal conservatism, liberal politics, and a compassionate heart." After having served six years in the military and thirty-four years working for a national corporation, he retired and now works as a commercial real estate broker. He's always been a person of faith, loyal to his church and living what he believed was a responsible Christian life.

One day a friend asked him to help transfer ownership of a very small frame house from a landlord to a farm worker family. It was the first time Jere had ever seen the way farm workers live, particularly if they are undocumented. As he got to know the family, he began to struggle to reconcile our current immigration issues with this family's needs and his personal value system. Here's the way Jere describes his conversation with God:

> Me: "God, I'm willing to do whatever you want me to do. Please help me understand your plan for me and how I might reconcile this immigration issue."
>
> God: "Well, there is something I want you to do, but first we need to correct a couple of your perceptions."

Over the next year and a half, a series of seemingly unrelated events began to happen in his life.

The Adult Education director at his church asked him to facilitate a small group using *A Disciple's Path*. As they made their way through the study, he found himself moving into a deeper understanding of what it might mean for him to love God with his whole heart, soul, mind, and strength, and to love his neighbor as he loved himself.

The Holy Spirit began to expand Jere's understanding of who his neighbor might be. Jere said, "My neighbor was no longer limited by a person's country of origin, legal status (documented or undocumented), or station in life. This expansion of thought added a new dimension—and desire—to my life that I needed to fulfill."

As he began his search for new ways to love God and serve his neighbor, God began sending people into his life "who either needed love or who were willing to offer love." He began to sense that he was being called to connect these two groups of people. As he began searching for how he might do that, he experienced more of what he calls "seemingly unrelated events that made no sense until later."

To understand immigration issues, he took an online course on "Immigration and US Citizenship." That was followed by an online course in Latin American culture.

As Jere continued his discipleship journey, the Holy Spirit began probing more deeply into his life.

- Did Jesus say, "Let the little children come unto me so that I can see if they are properly documented," or did he say, "Let the children come to me"?
- Did Jesus say, "I died on the cross to save only US citizens from the consequences of their sins" or did he say, "I died on the cross to save all from the consequences of their sins"?
- Which takes first priority in your life? Are you an American first? Or are you a Christian first?

At a civic luncheon Jere met a person who was already doing God's work in the migrant community. As they talked, Jere became energized by the opportunities to serve the academically talented migrant farm worker students and their families. Two high school graduates had been awarded scholarships, but their undocumented parents were unable to provide for other college expenses like transportation, clothing, food, and insurance.

As Jere began to visit the families in the migrant camps, he met other talented students and began to see what God was calling him to do. Along the way, God was sending him people from his church who were willing to share their love with these students and their families. Together they began responding to the opportunities before them by helping academically gifted students find their way to higher education.

At the time of this writing, they have supported twenty-six students who have attended ten different colleges and universities.

When winter came he learned that the children of the farm workers had no warm clothing, so this team worked with a local department store to supply winter clothing at a reduced cost. As word of the need spread, the community began to donate large quantities of blankets and warm clothing. He arranged for the Agape Food Bank to provide healthy food for 20 cents a pound. When a new baby was on the way, he arranged for a family to deliver the crib and baby supplies. When one student needed a cochlear implant, he found doctors and donors to make it happen.

Responding to God's call on his own life, Jere is also equipping other people who have limited amounts of flexible time to be involved in the ministry.

One businessman who has more than enough work to keep him busy gets up early every Wednesday morning to go to the Agape Food Bank where he picks up food that he and another volunteers deliver to migrant families. When asked why he does it, he said, "It comes from a place of passion and purpose. I work at my job to pay the bills, but this is where my heart is."

Jere laughs out loud when he says that he is having the time of his life connecting people who need love with people who offer love. "It is not about us. It's not even about the migrant students and their families. It's about God's love for us and our need to respond to His love for us." To visit the workers' homes with him is to experience the deep joy that only comes to those who follow their passion and find their place to serve. Jere has found the place where his great gladness and the world's great need meet.

Find Your Place to Serve

Responding to God's call to "Go where I send you" sent Jere to the migrant farm workers in central Florida. It took Albert Schweitzer to the middle of the African continent. It led Dietrich Bonhoeffer to confront the powers of Nazism in Germany and Desmond Tutu to oppose the powers of apartheid in South Africa. It inspired Congressman John Lewis to lead the march across the Edmund Pettus Bridge in Selma. But most of us won't become the next Schweitzer, Bonhoeffer, Tutu, or Lewis. Most of us are what Peter Marshall (1902-1949) called "saints of the rank and file."

As chaplain of the United States Senate, Marshall compared the Apostle Andrew, who is usually identified in the Gospel as "Simon Peter's brother," to "the man who sits beside you on the bus...drives the street-car...or waits on you in the store...or works at the next desk in your office." He described ordinary disciples as "the average men and women who are always taken for granted but without whom nothing could ever be accomplished.... They have a job to do, and they are willing to do it.... They have discovered the truth of the paradox of Christianity that only by losing one's life can one find it."[8] It's a description that fits every follower of Christ.

As everyday disciples, we all ask ourselves the same questions:

- Am I finding the place where the Lord is sending me?
- Am I open to the unexpected ways in which God might open my eyes to a specific need?
- Am I willing to change some of my assumptions about other people in order to be faithful to God's call for my life?
- Have I found a community of disciples to guide and support me?

When I was growing up, the powerful phrase, "Stop. Look. Listen" was painted on the X-shaped railroad crossing signs. Those three imperatives are good advice as we seek to find the place where we are called to serve. They also describe the way Moses experienced God's call.

The Old Testament storyteller said Moses was tending Jethro's flock when he *stopped* at Mount Horeb. That's where Moses *looked* at the burning bush. He *listened* and heard God say, "I've clearly seen my people oppressed in Egypt. I've heard their cry of injustice because of their slave masters. I know about their pain. I've come down to rescue them." Then Moses heard the Lord say, "So *get going*. I'm sending you to Pharaoh to bring my people…out of Egypt" (Exodus 3:3-10, esp. vv. 7-8, 10). Responding to that call, Moses became the agent of God's liberating power in the lives of his people.

Like Moses, we can discern where God is calling us to serve when we intentionally stop, look, and listen.

1. Stop!

Like Moses, most of us need to *stop* what we are doing in order to hear God's voice. When I surveyed a cross section of clergy and church members to identify the impediments that prevent people in their congregations from finding their place to serve, the most common answer was the pressure of time and over-commitment.

A young person in a rapidly growing suburban community replied, "Most people I know are overscheduled." A pastor in a growing church in one of the bustling suburbs of Johannesburg wrote: "Busy-ness: In the economic capital of South Africa, people live at a frenetic pace. Long commutes to work, juggling the demands of kids' extramural activities, mean that people jealously guard their 'downtime' and are hesitant to commit."

The last thing overly committed, hyperactive people need is for the church to add one more activity to their already-overloaded schedules. What the church can offer is the opportunity to stop the high-speed merry-go-round long enough to sort out the things that really matter and to set some clear priorities for their lives. Here are a few examples:

- One congregation encouraged their most active leaders to claim a season of "sabbath" during which they did not serve, so they could replenish their spirit.
- In another congregation, every class or small group was challenged to describe the way they were helping people set clear priorities to bring balance amid the demands of their careers, family responsibilities, and spiritual discipline.
- In other places churchwide retreats have focused on contemplation and prayer. One church offers a weekly time of centering prayer in their downtown chapel.
- A pastor in the mountains of North Carolina recommends taking church members backpacking on the Wilderness Trail. She described the way it separates people from the normal pressures of daily life and enables them to experience Christlike servanthood as they help one another along the trail. She writes, "It's been amazing for me to watch people be transformed by the experience, and then go home and transform their congregations by becoming models for others to imitate."
- Another congregational leader points to Bible study and other small-group studies as "a critical catalyst in getting people engaged in service. As people study the Scripture, learn about who God is, and catch a vision for God's saving purpose for creation, they have been invigorated to engage with the needs in the community."

If you are sharing this resource in a small group, the members of your group can help you identify specific ways to do this that are custom-designed for your community.

When John Ortberg was at a crossroad in his life, he asked a wise mentor for advice. His friend said, "You must ruthlessly eliminate hurry from your life." John quickly wrote the words down and asked, "What else?" The friend replied, "There is nothing else."[9]

Rather than add one more thing to an already overbooked, overachieving lifestyle, the church can begin by providing opportunities for faithful disciples to stop, take a deep breath, and be still in the presence of God. It's the only way to be ready for the next imperative.

2. Look!

When Moses *looked* at the burning bush he saw the suffering and pain of his people from the perspective of God's compassion and love. He was awakened by the fire of the Holy Spirit to see the injustice of the world in a whole new way. The first work of the Spirit in helping us to find our calling is to open our eyes so that we begin to see the world around us through the eyes of Jesus. Searching for and finding our places to serve involves looking with Spirit-awakened eyes at the needs of the world and at the gifts, talents, and opportunities we've been given.

The good news is that you don't have to see a burning bush or go on a mission trip to some distant part of the world for your eyes to be opened to the places where you can make a life-giving difference in the lives of others. The greatest value of that kind of experience is often the way it equips us to see more clearly the needs that are in our own backyard.

That's what happened for Jere Gault. As he visited the aging mobile homes in which migrant farm workers live, as he got to know their children, as he listened to the stories of their struggles with complex immigration issues, and as he searched for a way to link people needing love with people willing to offer love, his eyes were opened to the real hurts and hopes of real people. Problems about immigration and the needs of farm workers were no longer political issues to be debated but people to be served. His experience was similar to the way Moses, having been raised in the comfort and privilege of Pharaoh's palace, "went out among his people and he saw their forced labor." When Moses saw an Egyptian beating one of the Hebrew slaves, he suddenly realized that the slave was "one of his own people" (Exodus 2:11). It was as if their suffering under oppression became his own. When Moses *looked*, he began to see himself and people in need in a whole new way.

One of the unique challenges of our day is that it is frighteningly easy to live within a media-defined bubble. Many of us get all of our information about the world through the lens of a particular social, economic, and political perspective. We spent most of our time in racial and socioeconomic enclaves in which most of the people around us look, think, and act the way we do. We gravitate toward news sources that constantly reconfirm our preconceived assumptions. It's not that we are insensitive, mean, or bad people but that we are blinded by our own reflection in the mirror-like glass bowl in which we live. But disciples who hear God's call to make a difference in this world intentionally look at the world in a new and different way. They see the world through the lens of the infinite compassion and love of God. They look at people who are struggling and in pain as their "own people."

With Christlike eyes open to the world around us, we look then for the place where our strengths, talents, and availability connect with that need. Jere saw the way his past experience could be used by God to make a present and future difference in the lives of these people.

Pete Ferrara was a corporate executive in the communications business. When I asked why he feels a need to serve, he wrote, "Sometimes because I just 'want' to (I have a passion about someone or something) and other times because I feel I 'should' (guilt perhaps, it is the right thing to do)." He acknowledged that many programs within his church "don't sync up with either my skill set or my interests. If I am going to give my time, talent, or money I want it to be something I care passionately about. It is important to me that I can 'see' my participation and contribution make a difference."

He also pointed to his awareness of his gifts and experience. "At this point in my life, I pretty much know what I know and what I don't know. I have reasonably good understanding of what I am good at and what I am not. If I feel my involvement can really make a difference based on my experience and knowledge, I am not only willing to help, but honored to do so."

Connecting his passion, gifts, and availability led him to a continuing education program in which he serves on a panel of laypersons who are professionals in the communications business who help preachers understand how communication works (and what doesn't) in the world today.

My wife's passion is serving children. Her gift is teaching. She has never been called to join me on a mission team to South Africa where *Phakamisa*—the Zulu word for "uplift"—is providing preschools in the poverty-stricken townships around Durban. Her career calling was to serve children by teaching in public schools. After retiring, she has served in tutoring ministries for children from underprivileged neighborhoods.

Another retired teacher began a ministry that partners churches with schools in low-income neighborhoods and trains volunteers to serve as teacher assistants and math or reading coaches. This program inspired a faith-based initiative in the county public schools, which coordinates their "Adopt-a-School" program.

Another friend spent his career in politics as a member of the state legislature, a political consultant, and a lobbyist. Like these teachers, his passion is the welfare of children. He has used his political influence to make improvements in child protection services, children's health care, and public education.

After a career that began as a teacher in segregated public schools, in 1992, Doris Ross Reddick was elected as the first black woman to serve on the Hillsborough County School Board. She served for three terms, including one as chairperson of the board.

These United Methodist disciples shared a common passion for the needs of children, but as they looked at their skills, experience, and opportunities, they found distinctively different ways to make a difference in children's lives. When you look with Christlike compassion at the needs around you and look carefully at the gifts you have to offer, you will be ready to listen for God's call.

3. Listen!

The Exodus storyteller records, "When the Lord saw that he was coming to look, God called to him out of the bush, 'Moses, Moses!'" (Exodus 3:4). When Moses stopped and looked, he was in a position to hear the call of God. That call often comes through the urgency of the need that confronts us.

Frances Perkins (1880–1965) became the first woman to serve on the US Cabinet when FDR appointed her to be the secretary of labor in 1933. But her journey began as a teenager when she was confirmed in the Episcopal Church. She continued to practice the spiritual disciplines she learned in those years throughout her life. Even during the stressful twelve years she served in the government, she was regular in worship and reserved time for a monthly retreat for prayer and reflection with the Sisters of the Poor in Catonsville, Maryland. Through those disciplines, she learned to stop, look, and listen for God's call.

She was already engaged in the needs of the poor in New York City when the Triangle Shirtwaist Factory went up in flames in 1911, killing

146 garment workers. There were no fire codes in the city at the time. There were no extinguishers, exits were locked, and fire ladders were unable to reach the upper stories of the building. The fire traumatized the city and became a "burning bush" moment in Perkins's life. David Brooks wrote, "Her own desires and her own ego became less central and the cause itself became more central to the structure of her life."[10] He described it as "a summoned life.... Perkins didn't so much choose her life. She responded to the call of a felt necessity."[11]

Help us, following her example, to contend tirelessly for justice and for the protection of all in need, that we may be faithful followers of Jesus Christ.
—Collect for Frances Perkins's Day[12]

Here's my promise to you. When we *stop*, *look*, and *listen* we will hear God summoning us through the needs of others to find our way to make a compassionate difference.

Our eldest daughter spent the first half of her career producing the news for the local NBC affiliate in Orlando. She moved into another arena in communications, but on the Sunday morning when the whole world was shaken by "breaking news" of the attack at the Pulse nightclub in Orlando, her former boss called. They needed a local producer to work with the NBC team from New York who would be broadcasting from the scene one block away from the nightclub.

Carrie felt called to leave her family to go to the scene. She lined up the people who would be interviewed on the news—survivors, witnesses, family members, and friends. As she listened to their stories, she had a clear sense that she was there to offer Christlike compassion in a terrifying and terrible situation. You could say that she had been summoned by necessity.

Get Going!

In their own unique way, each of the persons whose stories I've shared in this chapter heard God say, "Get going!" (Exodus 3:10). But nothing would have changed if they had not responded to that call by taking action. The purpose of the *stop-look-listen* railroad sign is not to keep us sitting along the railroad track but to let us know when it is time to go. After an intense debate with God in which Moses offered every excuse he could think of, the writer finally says, "Moses went" (Exodus 4:18). Moses took action. He obeyed God's call and went to Pharaoh. The rest is the focal story of God's liberation of the covenant people, but none of it would have happened if Moses had not taken action.

I sometimes wonder what would have happened if Moses had refused to go; if he had continued to hide behind his excuses and had settled back down to tending Jethro's sheep. I wonder who the next person might have been whom God would have called to become the liberator of his people. When you read the debate between God and Moses it becomes clear that there was no hesitation on God's part. God was determined to liberate the people. God's insistent command to Moses was, "Get going!" The only question was whether Moses would be the one to do it. But if he had not obeyed the call, Moses would have missed his opportunity to be a part of God's transforming work in this world. This might be a good time to ask some disturbing questions:

- Have you seen any burning bushes lately?
- What does it mean for you to stop, look, and listen for God's call?
- What action is God calling you to take in response?

The lay leaders of Trinity United Methodist Church in Gainesville, Florida, were confronted with a "burning bush" moment when Terry Jones, the pastor of the fifteen-member Dove World Outreach

Center about a mile away, threatened to burn copies of the Quran on the ninth anniversary of the 9/11 attacks. Their initial response was to ignore the hateful actions of a minuscule group on the extremist fringe of our culture. That was the church's approach when members of the equally tiny, equally extremist Westboro Baptist Church picketed military funerals at their church, at St. Augustine Roman Catholic Church, and at the Hillel Synagogue a few months earlier.

But when the news media picked up the story, the church leaders knew that the time for silence had passed. They were summoned by necessity to take a stand. They knew that to remain silent would have been to be complicit with evil. The lay leaders joined their senior pastor in publically declaring that racist, anti-Islamic hatred was a total contradiction of the gospel and incompatible with the love and compassion of Jesus Christ.[13]

But words were not enough. God was calling them, the way God called Moses, to take action. They joined the Gainesville Interfaith Forum that brought together leaders from the Hindu, Muslim, Jewish, and Christian faiths in order to foster understanding, mutual respect, and peace while celebrating the uniqueness of each faith tradition. Taking a positive stand in contrast to Jones's hatred and bigotry, the people of Trinity Church hosted a "Gathering for Peace, Understanding, and Hope." It combined activities for children to play together, an exhibition of cultural arts and crafts, food and music from around the world, and times of prayer for peace, hope, and understanding led by leaders of each of the faith traditions.

The gathering exceeded everyone's expectations. More than one thousand people from across the city participated in an evening that reverberated with laughter, hope, and joy. It launched continued work for understanding and cooperation among the diverse religious traditions in the hometown of one of Florida's largest universities. The ongoing impact of their witness will continue to make a difference in that community for years into the future.

Each of the persons whose stories I have shared in this chapter heard the Spirit of God saying, "Children, go where I send you." In their own unique way, they experienced a "burning bush" moment in which they heard God calling them to make a transformative difference in this world through their own unique talents, experiences, and opportunities. In Buechner's words, they found their place to serve where their great gladness and the world's great need met. The same God who called Moses is alive in our world today calling you to stop, look, listen, and then go to make a liberating difference in the lives of people in the community in which you live.

Table Talk

Welcome to the table! Whether you join us alone or in a small group, we invite you to use these words from our panel—both on and off camera—as a springboard for reflection and discussion.

JIM: Buechner said our place to serve is where our great gladness and the world's great need meet. That means our discipleship begins in the church but gets lived out in the world.

NICK: There is a wrestling there. Some people are just as clearly called to teach Sunday school as a person who's called to serve in the women's shelter.

LISA: There's room for both. If you're deeply invested in children's ministry within the church, how will that translate to investing in the lives of children in your neighboring schools? The two can go hand in hand together.

DJ: In a culture where 95 percent do not attend worship, a woman in our congregation sees her mission as riding the bus to work and finding somebody to invite. She brings these visitors in, sits with them, and introduces them to friends. It's humbling to the staff because she brings more people in than we do!

JIM: The point is to find where God is using your unique gifts to make a Kingdom-shaped difference.

LINDSEY: The church is a training ground, right? It's where we're formed; where we learn to build community with people who are different from us. If that never goes out into the world, though, it's like a caterpillar that dies in the cocoon and never stretches its wings to fly.

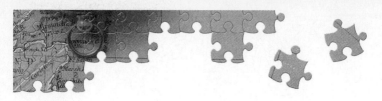

LISA: I think we have to push people sometimes and say, "Don't let the church become your place of comfort where you are never challenged to let your life overflow beyond the four walls."

LINDSEY: When we get motivated there's a temptation to burn ourselves out with busyness. I'd been doing work on the streets for more than ten years before I realized the call of Sabbath is not just recommended; it's a commandment. The other side of action is contemplation, and both are needed in the Christian life.

JIM: The railroad track is right outside the building where we are recording. The sound of it takes us directly to the crossing sign that calls us to stop, look, and listen.

LINDSEY: Thinking about stop, look, and listen, I think about my eyes and ears and what they're attuned to. I need to see outside of my location as a white Christian woman in America who is economically stable. I need to listen to my friends on the streets who are in survival mode. What can I learn from their experiences of trying to navigate a broken social services system, of trying to feed a family on food stamps? Points of transformation happen when we're listening to and learning across the things that polarize us. I'm trying to quiet myself down, so I can receive renewed and transformed—eyes, ears, and mind.

It's your turn. How will you join the conversation?

Questions for Reflection

- What do you need to do to *stop* the frantic pace of your life?
- When you begin to *look* with Christlike compassion at the world around you, what are the specific needs that call for your response? What are your talents and experiences that God might use to meet those needs?
- As you *listen* for the way God will lead you, what actions do you believe God is calling you to take in response?
- Where might the world's great need and your great gladness meet?

Prayer

Lord, make me an instrument of your peace:
where there is hatred, let me sow love;
where there is injury, pardon;
where there is doubt, faith;
where there is despair, hope;
where there is darkness, light;
where there is sadness, joy.

O divine Master, grant that I may not so much seek
to be consoled as to console,
to be understood as to understand,
to be loved as to love.
For it is in giving that we receive,
it is in pardoning that we are pardoned,
and it is in dying that we are born to eternal life.
Amen.
—Attributed to Saint Francis (1182–1226)

Lord, help me to find where the world's great need and my great gladness meet.
Amen.

Action Ideas

- Be intentional in taking Sabbath rest each week. In addition to spending time in prayer and worship, consider restful and renewing activities such as taking a walk or hike, enjoying nature, napping, and spending time with family and friends.
- Evaluate your priorities, identifying any areas where you need to make changes in order to address competing demands and make space for spiritual disciplines and service. Make notes in this book or a journal about anything you need to say no to, let go of, or take off your plate.
- Identify one need in "your own backyard" that you have the gifts, talents, experience, and opportunity to address. Plan a simple first step.
- Find a specific way you can connect with those outside your own racial and socioeconomic perspective. Listen to their stories and to how God might be calling you to respond.
- Spend some time identifying your gifts that might be used in service to others, either through a spiritual gifts assessment or simply by asking what unique talents, abilities, interests, and experiences you have. What opportunities do you see around you to use these gifts to make a difference?
- List those issues, concerns, or needs you are passionate about, as well as any related "burning bush" moments when you have sensed God calling you to get involved. Choose one and prayerfully consider a first or next step that God would have you to take. Discuss it with your small group or an accountability partner.

Chapter 4

GO TOGETHER

If you want to go fast, go alone. If you want to go far, go together.
—African proverb on the wall of the arrival gates of O. R.
Tambo International Airport, Johannesburg, South Africa

You may be surprised to learn that you have something in common with Hamlet. Even if you've never seen or read William Shakespeare's play, when you set out to make a difference in this world, you may be able to identify with the prince of Denmark when he told his best friend, Horatio: "The time is out of joint—O cursèd spite, / That ever I was born to set it right!"[1] Hamlet could see clearly the evil that surrounded him because of the deceit that led to the murder of his father. He knew he had been called to make things right. He was searching for a way to make a difference in a complex situation. Although you will probably not face the immensity of the evil that Hamlet confronted, when you feel called to help make things right in this world, you may be tempted to identify with his words. This can take shape in any number of ways:

- Your desire to make a Christlike difference has opened your eyes to some of the harsh realities of a world in which a lot of things are "out of joint." You know that things in this world aren't the way God wants them to be.
- Following your passion is making you more sensitive to the hurts and hopes of people around you. As you grow in your relationship with Christ, your heart is being broken by things that break the heart of God.
- Finding your place to serve may have uncovered complex challenges and intractable issues of power, injustice, racism, and evil that seem impossible to change.
- Fulfilling our mission of making disciples "for the transformation of the world" has turned out to be more complicated than you imagined.
- You still believe that "the light shines in the darkness, and the darkness doesn't extinguish the light" (John 1:5), but you are discovering that the world can still be a very dark and difficult place.

If you've made any of those discoveries, you might identify with Hamlet. You'd also be keeping company with the Old Testament psalmists and prophets who never hesitated to let God know their pain, frustration, and despair in their attempts to make a difference in their world. But the prince of Denmark went on to tell Horatio, "Nay, come, let's go together."[2] He knew he could not set things right by himself. Hamlet and Horatio needed to do it together.

Rinker Buck learned this lesson when he and his brother, Nick, set out to follow the Oregon Trail from St. Joe, Missouri, to Portland, Oregon, in 2011. Like the westbound pioneers in the nineteenth century, they did it in a covered wagon drawn by three mules.

Rinker spent two years planning every detail of the trip, including arranging for Nick to fly back East where he was committed to a community theater production. He was confident that he could make that portion of the journey alone until Nick would rejoin him a month later. But that confidence was brutally shattered by the challenges they faced along the trail. Driving and caring for the mules became more demanding than he had estimated. Nick was able to do critical repairs on the wagon that were beyond Rinker's ability. Steering the wagon through the mountains became as dangerous as it was difficult.

Rinker hated asking for help because it made him feel weak, and receiving help made him feel guilty. But as the time approached for Nick to leave, Rinker realized that he could not make the trip alone. Rinker wrote, "It was hard for me to be humble and say what I really felt then, but I knew that I had to." He finally acknowledged, "I do need you, Nick. I can't get across the trail without you." Nick replied, "We need each other....We're doing this together." To Rinker's surprise, Nick had already sent the message to his friends back East saying that he would not be coming. With a sigh of relief, Rinker concluded, "A great burden had been lifted from me."[3]

Bishop Bruce Ough, the spiritual leader of The United Methodist Church in Minnesota and the Dakotas, made a similar observation in a personal conversation about the Methodists who are scattered out across the Great Plains. He told me, "We have our differences, but we've inherited a frontier mentality in which we know that we are in this together, and we need to help each other. On the frontier, there was no room for wasting time and energy on things that really didn't matter very much." It's really true wherever we live. In an era when political polarization and ideological division seem to be the norm in both our culture and the church, we need a frontier mentality that reminds us that we're in this together.

Don't Try It Alone

When we set out to participate in God's transformation of the world, we soon discover that we can't do it alone. The challenges are too big, the injustice is too entrenched, the evil is too pervasive, and our individual efforts are too inadequate to think we could set things right on our own. The good news is that we don't have to! God never intended for any of us to make the long journey toward justice, reconciliation, and peace on our own. God intends for us to make a difference together.

You may not recognize their names, but Shiphrah and Puah were two seemingly insignificant women who were used by God to undermine the power of Pharaoh and set the work of salvation in motion at the beginning of the Book of Exodus. They were Hebrew midwives who received a direct command from the king of Egypt: "When you are helping the Hebrew women give birth and you see the baby being born, if it's a boy, kill him. But if it's a girl, you can let her live." At risk to their own lives, they "respected God so they didn't obey the Egyptian king's order. Instead, they let the baby boys live." Their bold act of civil disobedience meant that the people of Israel "kept on multiplying and became very strong" and ultimately led to the survival of a baby boy named Moses (Exodus 1:16-20, esp. vv. 17, 20).

By refusing to obey the king, two ordinary midwives helped give birth to a whole new world of possibilities for God's work of liberation in the face of overpowering oppression. Their decision to be obedient to God rather than the king helped undermine the power of the Egyptian empire. They modeled the way of faithful disobedience that continues to disrupt and threaten the powers of oppression and injustice in our world today. They are a biblical reminder of the way God works through marginalized or seemingly powerless people. It's an example of the way God chooses "what the world considers weak to shame the strong...what the world considers low-class and low-life...to reduce what is considered to be something to nothing" (1 Corinthians 1: 27-28). But I seriously doubt that either Shiphrah or Puah would have disobeyed the king's command alone. My guess is that they knew they would be stronger together.

The Oscar-nominated motion picture *Hidden Figures* brought to life the previously hidden story of the African American women who worked as mathematicians at NASA in the 1960s. The central character, Katherine Coleman Goble Johnson, grew up in the then-segregated St. James Methodist Church in White Sulphur Springs, West Virginia. At NASA, she led the team of women who broke through the barriers of sexism and racism and contributed to progress in both space travel and racial justice. Like Shiphrah and Puah, the NASA women did it together.

When Jesus commissioned seventy-two of his followers to go ahead of him, he knew that the task would not be easy. He warned them that "the harvest is bigger than you can imagine" and that he was sending them out "as lambs among wolves." Because he knew they would be stronger together, he "sent them on ahead in pairs" (Luke 10:1, 3). During the Last Supper, when Jesus reminded his disciples of their responsibility to go and produce fruit, he said, "I don't call you servants any longer....Instead, I call you friends" (John 15:15-16). With those words, Jesus transformed human friendship into a sacrament. It became the finite and tangible expression of an infinite and intangible grace. As disciples of Jesus Christ, we do not go into this world alone; we are bound together with friends who share a central commitment to Christ and a relentless passion to make a Kingdom-shaped difference in this world. We do it together.

A woman in Kampala, Uganda, came to Becca Stevens in search of support from Thistle Farms for a farming project there. It was clear to Becca that this woman was a capable farmer and talented entrepreneur who loved the land and had a compelling vision for social enterprise and feeding programs. What she needed was "a friend with some resources in the hard work of justice farming." Becca wrote, "We became friends that day. I learned from her and felt the joy of kinship....Everyone in the work of justice needs more friends."[4]

From the Oregon Trail to Uganda, from Genesis to the gospel and from Hamlet to Jesus, the lesson is the same. When we set out to make a difference, we soon discover that we cannot do it alone. We need to do it with a team of people who share the same passion and are finding their way to serve together.

> The physical presence of other Christians is a source of incomparable joy and strength to the believer....It is grace, nothing but grace, that we are allowed to live in community.
> —Dietrich Bonhoeffer[5]

Annette Colwell helped me learn this lesson in my first pastoral appointment. The church hosted a weekday school for mentally and physically challenged preschool children from low-income families, most of whom did not have transportation to bring their children to the church. Some of the children had to be carried from the car to the classroom. Annette served on a team of United Methodist Women who provided transportation to and from the school every day of the week. Married to a nationally recognized New Testament scholar, Annette had a brilliant mind and had been an active participant in the academic and social life of the schools and communities they had served prior to their retirement. I was always energized by conversations with her. One morning we arrived at the church at the same time. When I tried to engage her in conversation, she let me know in no uncertain terms that she didn't have time to talk that day. The other member of her team was unavailable, so Annette was driving the car and caring for the children on her own. She didn't need my conversation; she needed me to pick up a child and join her team!

Moses learned the importance of teamwork from his father-in-law, Jethro. Moses was working himself to exhaustion. From morning to night, people were standing in line all day to see him. Jethro, who could have earned a Harvard MBA in organizational management, began with the kind of question a business consultant might ask of an overworked executive, "Moses, why are you doing this all by yourself?" Like many highly-motivated leaders, Moses was a little defensive. "Are you kidding? The people keep coming and I'm the only one around here who can help them" (Exodus 18:14-16, author's paraphrase).

But Jethro offered a different analysis. He spoke the hard truth that Moses needed to hear. "What you are doing isn't good. You will end up totally wearing yourself out, both you and these people who are with you. The work is too difficult for you. You can't do it alone" (Exodus 18:17-18). Jethro laid out a plan for a decentralized organizational structure and promised, "This will be much easier for you, and they will share your load. If you do this and God directs you, then you will be able to endure. And all these people will be able to go back to their homes much happier" (Exodus 18:22-23).

The apostles needed to learn Jethro's lesson, too. The early Christian movement was growing so quickly that the apostles couldn't handle it. The result was that widows were being neglected in the daily distribution of food. So, the disciples appointed a team composed of Stephen and six other members to be responsible for the feeding ministry. As a result, "God's word continued to grow. The number of disciples in Jerusalem increased significantly" (Acts 6:7).

The point of these examples is that Christ-followers who try to set things right in this world have learned not to try to do the work alone; they do it together. It's a lesson that well-intentioned but overworked pastors need to learn, along with congregations that expect their clergy to do ministry for them. In his letter to Ephesus, Paul is clear that God's "purpose was to equip God's people for the work of serving and building up the body of Christ" (Ephesians 4:12). We're all in this work together.

Do the Good Stuff

A preacher friend told the story of a guy who was totally outside the faith, unrelated to any church, and spent most of his time high on drugs. By a miraculous series of events, he began reading the New Testament, particularly the Book of Acts. As he saw the way the Holy Spirit transformed the lives of those first followers of Christ, he found the power to break free from his addictions. He wanted to be like those early Christians and to be a part of a congregation that impacted their community the way the early church impacted the world in which they lived.

The first congregation he visited was a "rocking chair church" filled with kind-hearted, well-intentioned "rocking chair disciples." They were comfortably rocking back and forth, giving the illusion that they were going somewhere when, in fact, they were simply biding their time. They were doing the same things they had always done in the same ways they had always done them without much excitement or passion. Rather than a team of friends, they appeared to be a gathering of isolated individuals.

The recovering addict asked the pastor, "When do we get to the good stuff?" The bewildered pastor asked what he had in mind. The new believer said, "All that stuff in the Book of Acts about people going out to change the world." The pastor replied, "This is about all we do around here." To which the converted addict said, "You mean I gave up drugs for this?"

Based on his reading of the Book of Acts, that new disciple knew that there's more to life as a disciple of Jesus Christ than sitting in a pew on Sunday morning, being a nice person, and adding a little religion to our résumé. He sensed that the church has been called to the great task of being the living expression of God's kingdom. And he realized that this task is so big that it cannot be accomplished by a mere gathering of isolated individuals. He knew that being in community with other disciples was the only way the early Christians were equipped to accomplish the mission Jesus had given them and to make a transformative difference in the world. He was looking for "the good stuff" that only happens when followers of Christ are bound together in Spirit-energized service to others. Luke paints a wonderful picture of the way the early Christians shared their lives together:

> *The believers devoted themselves to the apostles'*
> *teaching, to the community, to their shared meals,*
> *and to their prayers. A sense of awe came over everyone.*
> *God performed many wonders and signs through*
> *the apostles. All the believers were united and shared*
> *everything. They would sell pieces of property and*
> *possessions and distribute the proceeds to everyone who*
> *needed them. Every day, they met together in the temple*
> *and ate in their homes. They shared food with gladness*
> *and simplicity. They praised God and demonstrated*
> *God's goodness to everyone. The Lord added daily to the*
> *community those who were being saved.*
>
> *(Acts 2:42-47)*

Luke's picture of the early Christian community captures some critically important practices of their life together that continue to be the transformative factors for our teamwork today. They shared an uncommon mission, they centered their common life in an uncommon ritual, and they practiced an uncommon generosity. Let's look at each of these practices separately.

1. Commit to an (Un)Common Mission

The early Christians were ordinary, imperfect people who were used by God to make a revolutionary difference in the first century because they were united in a shared commitment to an uncommon, exceptional mission. Their life together was centered in the words and story of Jesus that were passed on through the apostles' teaching. They were bound together in the command they had received from the Risen Christ: "Go and make disciples of all nations, baptizing them in the name of the Father and of the Son and of the Holy Spirit, teaching them to obey everything that I've commanded you" (Matthew 28:19-20).

With the fiery infusion of the Holy Spirit on Pentecost, they experienced the fulfillment of Jesus' promise: "You will receive power when the Holy Spirit has come upon you, and you will be my witnesses in Jerusalem, in all Judea and Samaria, and to the end of the earth" (Acts 1:8).

A quick reading of the Book of Acts reveals that they had a common commitment to an uncommon mission that was big enough and strong enough to bind them together when the differences between them threatened to tear them apart.

A visit to Monticello reminded me of the way Thomas Jefferson and John Adams became alienated from each other in the years following the American Revolution. They were reunited not long before both of them died on July 4, 1826, the fiftieth anniversary of the Declaration of Independence. In one of his letters to his old friend, Jefferson wrote:

> A letter from you...carries me back to the times when, beset with difficulties and dangers, we were fellow-laborers in the same cause, struggling for what is most valuable....Laboring always at the same oar, with some wave ever ahead threatening to overwhelm us...we rode through the storm with heart and hand, and made a happy port.[6]

Their common mission overcame their political conflicts, not unlike the way the early Christians were bound together in the uncommon mission they had received from Jesus Christ.

There have been differences and divisions in the church since the events recorded in the Book of Acts. The account of the Jerusalem Council in Acts 15 demonstrates the way the apostles resolved divergent interpretations of Scripture regarding the Jewish law that required circumcision, which Peter acknowledged was "a burden...that neither we nor our ancestors could bear" (Acts 15:10). The council came to a "united decision" that "the Holy Spirit has led us to the decision that no burden should be placed on you other than these essentials" (Acts 15:25, 28). Were it not for the action of that council, the fledgling Jesus movement might have been constrained within the boundaries of their Jewish tradition. But because they allowed diversity of practice around the circumference of the strongly held central mission, the witness of the gospel expanded exponentially to include the Gentile world. The mission they held in common was strong enough to keep people with equally strong but differing convictions in community with one another.

My pastoral experience has confirmed that when a congregation is centered in a clear, compelling, and commonly held mission, faithful disciples can handle diversity of conviction about practices that are on the circumference of their life together. The mission that unites them is stronger than the differences that would divide them.

John Wesley described this pattern of life when he said, "Though we cannot think alike, may we not love alike? May we not be of one heart, though we are not of one opinion? Without all doubt, we may. Herein all the children of God may unite, notwithstanding these smaller differences. These remaining as they are, they may forward one another in love and in good works."[7]

At the center of the Methodist movement was Wesley's focus on God's extravagant love for us and on Jesus' call for us to love God and love others. My observation is that where local congregations are intentionally living into that center of love and energetically engaged in our mission of "making disciples of Jesus Christ for the transformation of the world," great things are happening in amazingly diverse settings. A look across The United Methodist Church in the state where I live provides vibrant examples.

At First Church in Miami, it means making disciples and transforming the world among Cuban exiles and Haitian refugees.

At St. John's on Miami Beach, it means making disciples and transforming the world with a predominantly LGBTQ community.

At Trinity in Gainesville it means making disciples and transforming the world among millennial university students in a community with vibrant interreligious dialogue.

At First Church in Okeechobee it means making disciples and transforming the world with migrant farm workers and family farmers who are watching the Florida orange groves disappear.

At Hyde Park in Tampa it means making disciples and transforming the world with upwardly mobile professionals and their families.

At Covenant United Methodist in The Villages it means making disciples and transforming the world with predominately white retirees.

And that's just in Florida! Expand that picture across the United States and around the world and you catch a glimpse of the Spirit working with amazingly diverse people in equally diverse settings. But with all of our diversity, we are bound together by an uncommon mission we hold in common: to make disciples of Jesus Christ for the transformation of the world. Here are a few practical steps to help us stay united in our mission:

- Own the mission. It is not enough to simply accept the words and post them on a bulletin board. You and your team need to engage in regular Bible study and prayerful reflection on the church's mission, as well as your own faith community's mission, so that each person on the team can take personal ownership of it and participate in the constant renewal of it.

- Reaffirm the mission. The truth is that mission tends to leak. What is commonly assumed can easily be forgotten. For the mission to be the centrifugal center around which our community life revolves, we need to be constantly reminded of why we do what we are doing. One possibility is to begin every gathering with a clear restatement of your mission to remind everyone why you are here.

- Use the mission. Every time you make a decision about a plan of action, return to the mission and ask, "How does this particular decision help us fulfill our mission?" There is an almost infinite array of possible ways for faithful disciples to make a difference. Being faithful to the mission will inevitably mean saying no to many good things you could be doing so that you can say yes to the things that will make the most lasting difference in fulfilling your mission.

- Celebrate the mission. Rejoice together every time you see the mission being accomplished in your life together. Tell the stories of the way God's Spirit has been at work in and through your life together.

- Update the mission. As circumstances change around you, go back to the mission and ask, "How do the changes in our community impact the way we fulfill our mission?"

The early church made a seismic difference in human history because they poured their energy into fulfilling the uncommon mission that they held in common. They also shared an uncommon ritual.

2. Observe an (Un)Common Ritual

Every team, organization, or movement shares common rituals that reinforce their identity and mission. Those rituals are uncommon to people outside the group, but they give strength to those who practice them. For example, a visitor to a University of Florida football game may be surprised at the end of the third quarter when, without announcement, the Gator fans stand up, wrap their often-sweaty arms around one another's shoulders, and sway back and forth as they sing "We Are the Boys of Old Florida." They've been doing it for generations. The ritual is so deeply imbedded in their culture that an attempt at more inclusive language was promptly defeated.

Looking in from the outside, people must have been surprised by the uncommon ritual that the early Christians held in common. Those first meals they shared together became the Eucharist. It became the shared ritual that held them together, defined their identity, and empowered them for service. Paul said he passed on the tradition he had received from the Lord through the practices of the early church.

On the night on which he was betrayed, the Lord Jesus took bread. After giving thanks, he broke it and said, "This is my body, which is for you; do this to remember me." He did the same thing with the cup, after they had eaten, saying, "This cup is the new covenant in my blood. Every time you drink it, do this to remember me." Every time you eat this bread and drink this cup, you broadcast the death of the Lord until he comes (1 Corinthians 11:24-25).

Eugene Peterson described the Eucharist ritual as "the definitive action practiced in the Christian community that keeps Jesus Christ before us as the Savior of the world." He warned that when the Eucharist is not our "focal practice," we can easily imagine Jesus as the "Great Example whom we will imitate, or our Great Teacher from whom we will learn, or our Great Hero by whom we will be inspired." Instead, the communion ritual "puts Jesus in his place: dying on the cross and giving us that sacrificed life. And it puts us in our place: opening our hands and receiving the remission of our sins, which is our salvation."[8]

The Wesley brothers placed the Eucharist at the center of our life together in the Methodist tradition. In his sermon "The Duty of Constant Communion," John Wesley described the sacrament as "food of our souls" that "gives strength to perform our duty, and leads us on to perfection."[9] Don't miss the way Wesley saw the ritual of Holy Communion as the source of strength for the fulfillment of our calling. Consistent with that tradition, the United Methodist communion liturgy prays:

> Pour out your Holy Spirit on us gathered here,
>   and on these gifts of bread and wine.
> Make them be for us the body and blood of Christ,
>   *that we may be for the world the body of Christ,*
>   redeemed by his blood.
>
> By your Spirit make us one with Christ,
>   one with each other,
>   and *one in ministry to all the world,*
>   until Christ comes in final victory
>   and we feast at his heavenly banquet.

After receiving, we conclude by praying together:

> Eternal God, we give you thanks for this holy mystery
>   in which you have given yourself to us.
> Grant *that we may go into the world*
>   *in the strength of your Spirit,*
>   *to give ourselves for others,*
>   in the name of Jesus Christ our Lord. Amen.[10]

Notice the strong emphasis in those prayers on way the sacrament empowers us to be the agents of God's love in the world. It is the ritual that binds us together and then sends us out from the table to find our way to serve.

As the central ritual of our life together, the sacrament also provides the pattern by which Jesus' followers are sent out to transform the world. In Luke's account of the Last Supper, Jesus' action is described by four verbs that also define the way we are sent to serve: "He *took* bread, *blessed* and *broke* it, and *gave* it to them" (Luke 24:30 NRSV, emphasis added).

Jesus took the ordinary, unleavened bread, waiting on the table to be eaten during the Passover meal, and designated it as the sign of his body that would be broken as the ultimate expression of God's transforming love. He took an ordinary cup of wine, and named it as the sign of his blood, poured out in extravagant love for the whole world. He blessed those ordinary gifts, broke them, and gave them to his disciples.

In the same way, the Spirit of God takes, blesses, breaks, and gives the ordinary gifts and talents that we offer. There's a word here for anyone who is tempted to believe that they have little or nothing to give; that their lives can never really make a difference; that their service doesn't really matter. God doesn't call us to be anyone other than who we are or to give something we don't already have. The Spirit takes the ordinary stuff of our very ordinary lives, blesses us, breaks us, and gives us to the world as the extraordinary sign of God's infinite love.

Don't discount the ordinary gifts in your life that God can use in an extraordinary way. In the same way that God took the ordinary shepherd's staff in Moses' hand (Exodus 4:17) and Jesus took, blessed, broke, and gave the ordinary gifts on that Passover table, God is able to take whatever we have in our hands and use it for a Kingdom purpose.

Stephen Crawford had served on just about every leadership committee in the church. He was faithful in worship, sang in the choir, participated in a Sunday school class, and was always willing to do whatever was needed to support the church. But he was still searching for the way he could make a difference beyond the walls of the church. As a criminal defense attorney, he had not fully realized that God could use his talent and experience in the lives of the people he represented. He sensed the Spirit of Christ with him in the way he related to his clients and tried to offer hope to people who were facing difficult and severe challenges. His work didn't change. He didn't start preaching or handing out Bibles to the people he defended. But something about the way he listened to their stories and did what he could to help them began to feel like a finite expression of the compassion of Christ that is portrayed in breaking the bread and sharing the cup of communion.

When he became engaged in his congregation's ministry with homeless people, he discovered the place where his great gladness and the world's great need came together. Not unlike the way Jesus called the disciples his friends as they gathered around the Passover table, he became a friend to people from the streets as he joined them around the breakfast tables. He used his leadership gifts to help organize the volunteers to serve and keep the ministry running smoothly. His experience with police and the legal system enabled him to handle some of the behavioral and legal challenges among the people they served. It ignited his passion and confirmed that this was the way the Spirit of Christ could take, bless, break, and use the ordinary stuff of his life in Christlike service to others.

3. *Practice an (Un)Common Generosity*

The uncommon generosity of the early church is just as uncommon today as it was in the first century. The extravagant generosity described in Acts 2 becomes practical action two chapters later.

> *"The community of believers was one in heart and*
> *mind. None of them would say, 'This is mine!' about*
> *any of their possessions, but held everything in*
> *common.... There were no needy persons among*
> *them. Those who owned properties or houses would*

> *sell them, bring the proceeds from the sales, and*
> *place them in the care and under the authority of the*
> *apostles. Then it was distributed to anyone who was*
> *in need."*
>
> *(Acts 4:32, 34-35)*

There is debate about how long this form of communal economics continued in the early church, but there is no debate about the spirit of generosity that lay behind it. In a culture that is largely driven by unmitigated, self-serving greed, the distinguishing mark of discipleship in our age will undoubtedly be the ways in which we demonstrate an uncommon generosity that is a direct extension of the extravagant, self-giving generosity of God.

Politicians of every persuasion are quick to quote John Winthrop's vision of our nation as a "city on a hill." They are not as quick to refer to the rest of his sermon "A Model of Christian Charity," written onboard the *Arabella* as its passengers prepared to arrive on this continent in 1630. It was consistent with Luke's description of the early Christian community:

> "We must be knit together, in this work, as one man.... We must be willing to abridge ourselves of our superfluities, for the supply of others' necessities. We must uphold a familiar commerce together in all meekness, gentleness, patience and liberality. We must...make others' conditions our own; rejoice together, mourn together, labor and suffer together, always having before our eyes our commission and community in the work, as members of the same body. So shall we keep the unity of the spirit in the bond of peace."[11]

The generosity of the early church upon which Winthrop based his vision of a generous community continues to be a distinguishing characteristic of the way we are called to live together. It is the way we fulfill Jesus' promise, "This is how everyone will know that you are my disciples, when you love each other" (John 13:35). As Winthrop made clear, it is not only with financial generosity, but the lavish generosity with which we welcome, forgive, support, and care for one another. It is also the way we give ourselves in service to the world.

There is a gold chalice on the altar at St. Mary's (Episcopal) Convent in Tennessee. It is a eucharistic symbol of the kind of extravagant generosity to which followers of Christ are called. In 1873, four Sisters of Mary were sent to Memphis to begin a school for girls and a home for the poor. The work was interrupted by the yellow fever epidemic of 1878. Nearly the entire population either died or fled the city. Even though they had no formal training as nurses, the four sisters stayed in the city to care for the sick and dying. Three of the sisters died in the epidemic and are remembered in the Episcopal Church as the "Martyrs of Memphis." In 1888, when Hughetta Snowdon, the only surviving sister, moved to the mountains to start a new branch of the order, she brought the chalice with her. It sits on the altar today as a witness to the extravagant generosity of the sisters who gave their lives in extraordinary and loving service to people in need.[12]

You will probably not be called to give your life the way the Martyrs of Memphis gave theirs, but every disciple who makes a Christlike difference in this world is called to the same spirit of uncommon generosity. Their witness challenges us to find our own uniquely uncommon way to live generously in Christian community so that we can be strengthened to give ourselves generously to the world around us.

The "good stuff" that we see in the Book of Acts continues to be a reality among followers of Christ who know that the only way to make a difference in this world is to do it together—followers like Dorothy Lieving who followed her passion, found her place to serve, and built a team that could carry out her mission.

It would have been difficult to miss the dozen or so homeless men who used to line up across the street from Hyde Park United Methodist Church on Sunday morning. They waited for the congregation to go into the sanctuary for worship so they could come into the courtyard for a cup of coffee or a glass of orange juice. Dorothy not only saw them, she got to know them. She knew their names and became familiar with their stories. One Sunday she decided to bring peanut butter and jelly sandwiches to go with their coffee. That began the sandwich ministry.

Dorothy knew that freezing the bread made the peanut better easier to spread, so every Saturday night she put the loaves of bread in the freezer. The next morning as she made the sandwiches, she would pray for the person who would receive that one. Her sandwiches became a tangible expression of God's love for each one of them.

As the number of homeless or near-homeless men, women, and children grew, other members of the congregation joined Dorothy's team. Dorothy created a spreadsheet to coordinate the volunteers who agreed to pray for the people as they made the sandwiches. As more people joined the team, the menu began to expand, too. Some brought fruit; some brought other baked goods.

When the congregation moved into their new activities center, the leaders of the "Peanut Butter Buddy" team asked if they could invite their guests to come inside for breakfast. The church's food service manager began bringing out the leftovers from last Wednesday night's dinner. Sometimes he would cook a full breakfast with sausage and eggs. One team member went to a local restaurant early every Sunday morning to pick up their day-old bread. The ministry continued to grow with more volunteers bringing their own unique talents. Some provided haircuts; another offered legal advice; another connected with a mobile dental service; others developed a clothes closet. Along the way, those who came for breakfast became real people to those who served.

The "Peanut Butter Buddies" began with one disciple responding to a specific need. But if Dorothy had continued doing it alone, the ministry would have died with her. Instead, by the time Dorothy died, her individual sandwich ministry had grown into the "Open Arms Ministry" that involves nearly four hundred volunteers and serves approximately two hundred persons every Sunday morning.

It's a tough world out there! If we try to make a difference on our own, we can easily become frustrated and want to quit. The transformation of the world is far too big and far too complex a mission for any of us to accomplish on our own. But we are not called to be solo performers. Ministry in the body of Christ is always a team sport. We need the strength, wisdom, and accountability of a community to fulfill our calling. We follow our passion and find our place to serve in community with other disciples. We go into the world together.

Table Talk

Welcome to the table! Whether you join us alone or in a small group, we invite you to use these words from our panel—both on and off camera—as a springboard for reflection and discussion.

JIM: Jesus didn't call us to do life alone. How do we live in community and how does life in community become the expression of the kingdom of God?

DJ: Where I serve, we have a growing percentage of nondominant people, of tribal cultures. It's forced us to see our calling through the lens of others—folks from Russia, Korea, Africa. Our calling is not individualistic anymore.

NICK: I'm not sure I would have considered the directions I've gone if it hadn't been for people who spoke into my life when I wanted to quit or go in other directions. The community both instigates and sustains the call.

JIM: I screw up enough when I have a community around me, but I really screw up when I try to do it on my own! The more we try to follow God's call, the more we know how much we need one another.

LISA: I have more fun when I'm not going alone. To have someone we can celebrate the win together, for a person to encourage or to offer up words of blessing when you don't think your hands are capable of doing the thing. It's just way more fun to high-five another person than to high-five yourself.

LINDSEY: We couldn't do the work we do without attorneys, doctors, educators, people who have gifts we don't. Maybe I'm on the front lines today and others are supporting me and you're on the front lines tomorrow and I'm supporting you.

JIM: There are things that I would be afraid to try on my own. I never would have gone out on the streets in Johannesburg at night alone. But when they said, "We're going together," I knew that I could trust them and I went.

LINDSEY: Servant leadership can mean stepping back and making space for people who might not be used to leading but have those gifts, and to draw those out. Working on the streets, we're trying to make ourselves small and let the gifts and the voices of the people rise up so that their leadership can fill in this vacuum. People have gifts that haven't been realized because they've been shot down because they're poor or they're not white or because they have a learning disability.

DJ: I think leadership at its best empowers others to find their own voice and allows a voice that is not the same as mine to be heard and not wait for his or her or their own time to speak.

LISA: When folks get a taste of life together and see some miracle break forth because they're serving together, they never want to go back to the old life of trying to do it alone.

It's your turn. How will you join the conversation?

Questions for Reflection

- Who sees the same need and shares the same passion that you feel?
- Where is God already at work to meet this need? How can you get on board with what God is already doing?
- What can you learn from people who have tried to meet this need before?
- How can you build a Spirit-energized team that will sustain the ministry over time?
- How are you practicing the uncommon practices of the early church? Where have you experienced an uncommon mission, an uncommon ritual, and an uncommon generosity? How have those practices helped you make a difference?

Prayer

All praise to our redeeming Lord,
who joins us by His grace,
and bids us, each to each restored,
together seek His face.

He bids us build each other up;
and, gathered into one,
to our high calling's glorious hope,
we hand in hand go on.
—Charles Wesley[13]

Lord, direct my steps as I follow my passion to join my brothers and sisters in Christ in serving others for the transformation of the world. Amen.

Action Ideas

- Participate in Holy Communion as part of your regular life in Christian community—not only in corporate worship but also in small groups and ministry teams. Periodically invite a pastor to serve the elements in a group session or before a service or ministry effort.
- Invite people who share a passion for a need you see to share a meal and explore how you might work together to meet this need. Discuss what you can do to join in what God is already doing, to learn from others, and to build a Spirit-energized team for ongoing ministry.
- List ordinary gifts (your own or those of others) that you have seen God use in extraordinary ways. Consider how you might use an ordinary gift this week to serve in/beyond your faith community.
- Prayerfully reflect on the church's mission as well as the mission of your own faith community. Consider committing them to memory. Look for ways your church body is accomplishing its mission and how you might contribute, and let go of any differences that threaten to divide you.
- Choose a specific way to practice extravagant generosity in your faith community—whether by giving, welcoming, forgiving, supporting, or caring for others.

Chapter 5

INTO THE CRUCIBLE
OF PAIN AND HOPE

If you want to know whether God is alive, you must go, not to where all is well, but into places of brokenness and suffering.... There are depths of reality, dimensions of God, releases of healing energy, that flow into the world only through the power of faithful suffering.

—*Peter Storey[1]*

This chapter comes with a warning. If you want your life to make a Christ-shaped difference in this world, it will inevitably mean going with Jesus into places you might otherwise want to avoid. Jesus wasn't exaggerating when he said that being his disciple involves taking up a cross and following him into very real places of human suffering and pain. The promise is that those are the places where your great gladness and the world's great need meet. By God's grace, the crucible of pain can become the place where hope is born.

Finding Hope When Words Won't Work

I work with words. As a preacher, words are my stock-in-trade, the standard equipment I use to fulfill my ministry. I am called to make a difference by using finite language to communicate infinite truth; touching a person's heart through what he or she hears. Across four decades in ministry, I've poured my time, energy, and prayer into attempting to wrap words around experiences or ideas that are too big, too mysterious, or too painful for words to contain. Along the way I've learned that there are times when language cannot carry the weight of what we feel. There are times when words won't work. You may have learned the same lesson. When tragedy strikes, when violence erupts, when injustice wins, when pain becomes palpable, or disappointment closes in like a thick fog around you, it may leave you at a loss for words.

The aftermath of the attack on the Pulse nightclub in Orlando was one of those times for residents of Central Florida and for people who followed the story across the nation. In the early hours of Sunday, June 12, 2016, forty-nine people died and fifty-three were wounded when a lone gunman entered the gay nightclub and began shooting. It was one of those times, like too many other times in our violence-addicted, gun-saturated culture, that fit two of Shakespeare's final lines in "King Lear":

> The weight of this sad time we must obey.
> Speak what we feel, not what we ought to say.[2]

But what words can carry the full weight of what we feel in pain-saturated, hate-soaked times like these? What can we say? What can we do? How can followers of Christ make a difference in places of injustice, pain, and suffering?

In times like these, I'm grateful for Paul's promise that the Holy Spirit "helps us in our weakness; for we do not know how to pray as we ought, but that very Spirit intercedes with sighs too deep for words" (Romans 8:26 NRSV). J. B. Phillips paraphrased that verse to say that God's own Spirit prays within us in "agonising longings which never find words."[3] John Bunyan (1628–88), the author of the Christian classic *The Pilgrim's Progress*, must have had Paul's words in mind when he wrote, "The best prayers have often more groans than words."[4]

The Old Testament prophet Jeremiah experienced that kind of groaning. He is often remembered as the "weeping prophet" because of the way he attempted to wrap words around his pain when he saw the suffering of his people and the fall of Jerusalem in 587 BC:

> *No healing,*
> > *only grief;*
> > > *my heart is broken.....*
> *Because my people are crushed,*
> > *I am crushed;*
> > > *darkness and despair overwhelm me.*
> > > > *(Jeremiah 8:18, 21)*

> *If only my head were a spring of water,*
> > *and my eyes a fountain of tears,*
> *I would weep day and night*
> > *for the wounds of my people.*
> > > *(Jeremiah 9:1)*

Those are the words of a God-centered person who walked the hard road of injustice, suffering, and pain with his people. His heart was broken by the things that broke their hearts and broke the heart of God.

Our identification with people who suffer is neither an insignificant nor an optional thing. By entering into another person's pain we are drawn into the presence of the God who came among us as the "suffering servant" in the prophecy of Isaiah (Isaiah 53:1-12). Paul went so far as to claim that he was "completing what is missing from Christ's sufferings with [his] own body" (Colossians 1:24). In the fourteenth century, a contemporary of Julian of Norwich wrote, "Christ and she were so united in love that the greatness of her love was the cause of the greatness of her pain."[5]

Our God is a suffering God....
Our joy is hidden in suffering....
Christians must drink the earthly cup
to the dregs, and only in doing so
is the crucified and risen Lord with them.
—Dietrich Bonhoeffer[6]

As disciples of Jesus Christ, we are called to join him in the crucible of pain, suffering, and injustice the way the Samaritan on his way to Jericho entered into the unjust suffering of the man he found along the side of the road. Making a difference in the lives of people who experience oppression, suffering, or injustice begins when we choose to enter into their experience, listen to their story, and join them in their pain. In the same way God's Son became one of us to share our human life, we are drawn closer to Jesus by drawing closer to people in pain.

Find Hope in the Place of Pain

The good news is that Paul doesn't leave us speechless in the place of pain. The word that makes a transformative difference when all other words fail is *hope*. A wise mentor taught me that the role of a redemptive leader is to name reality and to give hope. As the agents of God's healing love, we are called to empower and strengthen those who suffer, not with some sort of phony optimism but with God-centered, biblically rooted hope. Paul declared: "We were saved in hope. If we see what we hope for, that isn't hope. Who hopes for what they already see? But if we hope for what we don't see, we wait for it with patience" (Romans 8:24-25).

After acknowledging our groaning prayers, John Bunyan went on to say, "Hope has a thick skin, and will endure many a blow."[7] Thick-skinned hope is grounded in the assurance that God hasn't given up on us or on this creation. Our hope is that God is at work in the crucible of the injustice, pain, and suffering to fulfill the promise of that day when the kingdoms of this world actually will become the Kingdom of our God (Revelation 11:15). We lift up the hope that one day "He will wipe away every tear from their eyes. Death will be no more. There will be no mourning, crying, or pain anymore, for the former things have passed away" (Revelation 21:4). When other words won't work, the word that works is hope. Through his tears, Jeremiah announces that word of hope for his people.

> *The* LORD *proclaims:*
> *The people who survived the sword*
> *found grace in the wilderness....*
> *I have loved you with a love that lasts forever.*
> *And so with unfailing love,*
> *I have drawn you to myself.*
> *Again, I will build you up,*
> *and you will be rebuilt, virgin Israel.*

Again, you will play your tambourines
and dance with joy....
There's hope for your future.

(Jeremiah 31:2-4, 17)

Hope is the word that makes the difference, even in the darkest places of injustice and pain.

Paul's words about suffering and hope came alive for me during the time I spent in one of the sprawling townships and informal settlements on the outskirts of Johannesburg. Nearly a million people are crammed into small, concrete-block houses surrounded by tin shacks that spread across the veld. We engaged with teachers in tiny preschools that often provide the only meal the children will have that day. We visited in the homes of HIV/AIDS patients and the clinics that provide the medications they desperately need. I met a home health care worker who gave up her own food for patients who needed to eat before receiving their meds. I spent the night with a family who welcomed me into their modest home with exceptional warmth and hospitality.

Providentially, the lectionary readings for that week included Romans 8:18-38. My journal reflections captured the way the Scripture came alive to me that day:

> Lord, I've experienced "the sufferings of this present time" in the lives of Sofiso, Margaret, Tidimalo, Zoe, Nomaliso and James.
>
> Lord, you promise that one day these people will find the freedom you intend for all your children. We long for it, Lord, with groans too deep for words. The groaning in us is nothing less than the groaning of your Spirit.

While we wait, we have the first fruits of the future in our hands. We wait with active patience, praying that you are working for good through us.

Lord, the need is so large; the suffering so immense. I'd walk away if I could. But I remember Mamma Annie, giving herself to others with such joy. She is the sign of your hope. And here, in a place I would have avoided, I have found great love and strange joy. Thank you, Lord.

In places of pain, loss, and injustice, the people who make the difference are people who live out of a deep, relentless, and soul-strengthening gift of hope.

Salvation is free, but the cost of discipleship is enormous....To bind our lives to Jesus Christ requires that we try to walk with him into the sorrows and suffering of the world....We are led to places we have never been before and to carry loads we have not even seen before.
—Rueben Job (1928–2015)[8]

Experiencing a Bright Sadness

I saw hope again in a place of ruthless evil and painful suffering after the attack on the Pulse nightclub. The club was within walking distance of First United Methodist Church of Orlando. The 130-year-old urban center church that was once the largest congregation in Florida spent the past few years wrestling with its identity and mission in a rapidly changing city. It was a process of painful honesty, persistent prayer, and bold faith resulting in fresh clarity around their mission: "Seek and Love God. Love and Serve People." Living into that mission in the heart of Orlando has included welcoming a significant number of gay and lesbian disciples into their life and ministry. Longtime church members have built personal relationships through which they have heard stories of rejection, prejudice, fear, and hope in the lives of LGBT brothers and sisters in Christ.

When news of the Pulse attack broke, church leaders were stunned but not frozen in confused inaction. A longtime member and leader in the congregation said that because of the clarity of their mission, there was no question that they would find ways to respond to the pain, fear, and anguish that surrounded them. Evasion was impossible. The circumstances compelled their compassion. Discipleship demanded action. They could not be who God had called them to be and act as if nothing had happened around them. Living their mission meant opening the sanctuary for the people who crowded into the heart of the city later that day. She said it felt like "an almost automatic response to fulfill our mission. We knew we were in the right place at the right time." She said that the crisis forced them to ignore the petty differences that sometimes infect a congregation in order to find their way to serve.

On Monday after the attack, a massive candlelight vigil overflowed the city park across the street. Again, the church doors were open, the restrooms were available, and church members stood on the sidewalk offering bottled water, a listening ear, and a place for prayer. The church staff and lay leadership poured their time, energy, and resources into planning and leading an interfaith prayer service that included representatives of every religious tradition in the city. The church hosted the funeral for a person who was killed in the attack, providing a witness of welcome and compassion for people who had either rejected or been rejected by the church in the past. It reminded me of a seminary professor who told us that sometimes the church is called to be an enclave of heaven in the middle of hell.

And here's the grace-filled surprise. In a place of immense pain, people who had followed their passion and found their way to serve also experienced an incorrigible joy in knowing that God was using their ways of serving to bring healing and hope to shattered lives and a broken city. They experienced what Richard Rohr called "a bright sadness: you are sad because you now hold the pain of the larger world…but there is brightness because life is somehow—on some levels—still 'very good.'"[9] With Jeremiah, they found grace in the wilderness. Their ways of serving became a tangible expression of love and hope. The place of suffering became the crucible in which pain was transformed into hope. When a CBS News reporter asked Tom McCloskey, the lead pastor at First United Methodist, how he holds onto the hope that things will get better, he said, "My faith says that one day all will be equal."[10] That's hope with a tough skin.

I experienced the same "bright sadness" during my first visit to South Africa. Elizabeth Storey was the administrative assistant to Desmond Tutu when he led the South African Council of Churches in the struggle against apartheid. In that position, she was responsible for a fund that was available to bury people who lost their lives in detention and whose families could not afford a funeral. Day after day, Elizabeth listened to their stories and entered into their pain. Once I said to her, "That must have been very difficult for you." I can still see the gentle smile on her face and the deep warmth of her voice when she corrected me. "Oh no, Jim." She said, "I was privileged to share their pain."

David Brooks pointed toward a biblical truth when he wrote that "there is nothing intrinsically noble about suffering….Suffering is sometimes just destructive, to be exited or medicated as quickly as possible." But he observed the way "suffering simultaneously reminds us of our finitude and pushes us to see life in the widest possible connections, which is where holiness dwells." In that way, suffering can become "a fearful gift."[11]

Live with the Mind-set of Jesus

The question is, *how*? How do I enter into the pain, suffering, injustice, and brokenness of this world in a way that enables me to make a tangible, Christ-shaped, hope-energizing difference?

Paul answers that question by challenging us to live with the same attitude or mind-set as the one we see in Jesus (Philippians 2:5). He described Jesus' mind-set by lifting a hymn or affirmation out of the worship of the early Christian community.

> *Though he was in the form of God,*
> > *he did not consider being equal with God*
> > *something to exploit.*
> *But he emptied himself*
> > *by taking the form of a slave*
> > *and by becoming like human beings.*
> *When he found himself in the form of a human,*
> > *he humbled himself by becoming obedient to the*
> > *point of death,*
> > *even death on a cross.*
> *Therefore, God highly honored him*
> > *and gave him a name above all names,*
> *so that at the name of Jesus everyone*
> > *in heaven, on earth, and under the earth might bow*
> > *and every tongue confess that*
> > > *Jesus Christ is Lord, to the glory of God the*
> > > *Father.*
>
> *(Philippians 2:6-11)*

The hymn points to three transformative steps we can take along the way through pain toward hope: Jesus emptied himself, became a servant, and was obedient. Let's look at each one together.

1. Get Yourself Out of the Way

Jesus emptied himself. At the center of the Christian gospel is the astounding affirmation that the one who was equal with God emptied himself and became one of us. Charles Wesley said he "emptied himself of all but love."[13] The seventeenth-century Anglican priest and poet George Herbert painted a powerful visual image of this earth-shaking truth:

> The God of power, as he did ride
> In his majestic robes of glorie,
> Reserv'd to light; and so one day
> He did descend, undressing all the way.[14]

The great mystery of the Incarnation is that God's love in Christ is alive among us in the complex, conflicted, confusing mess of our ordinary lives and our broken world. It's not an esoteric flight from reality but a present experience in our very real world. The Incarnation is not just a doctrine to be believed but a mystery to be lived out in the hustle and bustle, the joy and pain, the power and the politics, the hope and despair of our lives each day.

Even as God's love became flesh among us in the self-emptying of Christ, we are called as his followers to make a difference in this world by becoming the self-emptying, flesh-and-blood agents of God's incarnate, reconciling love and grace in our own time and place. Paul combined God's work of reconciliation in the life, death, and resurrection of Jesus with our work of reconciliation in the world when he wrote:

*All of these new things are from God, who reconciled
us to himself through Christ and who gave us the
ministry of reconciliation. In other words, God was
reconciling the world to himself through Christ, by not
counting people's sins against them. He has trusted us
with this message of reconciliation.*

(2 Corinthians 5:18-19)

When it comes down to it, the mystery is not only that Christ emptied himself and came among us, but that God intends for us to be the continuing expression of that same self-emptying love in the lives of others. If we are to enter into the pain of others with the mind-set of Jesus, the first step is to empty ourselves, to undress ourselves of arrogant pride, to get our self-absorbed attitudes out of the way. It's what a courageously committed layman meant when he taught me to say, "This is so not about me."

Trevor Hudson remembers the moment in 1982 when he realized that the white members of his middle-class, suburban congregation were largely unaware of the effects of apartheid in South Africa. Even the highways that led from Johannesburg to Soweto were designed to shield white people from seeing the oppression of black people around them. They lived most of their lives in a bubble of comfort surrounded by an ocean of injustice and pain. The Spirit spoke to him with startling clarity, "Take members of your congregation with you to where their brothers and sisters are suffering."[15]

The "Pilgrimage of Pain and Hope" invited people to experience an eight-day immersion in the lives of suffering people, which resulted in profound spiritual transformation in the lives of those who participated. Both from observation of other pilgrims and from his own experience, Trevor came to the awareness that "my suffering neighbor is where I meet the crucified and risen Christ."[16] The key to the experience was that they went "as pilgrims, not as tourists; as learners, not as teachers; as receivers, not as givers; as listeners, not as talkers."[17]

Emptying oneself means laying aside the need to be in control, to have all the answers, and to be the one who comes to fix things. It means learning to listen deeply with openness to whatever the Spirit of God might have to teach us in that time and place. It calls for humility. Becca Stevens learned that the key to getting ourselves out of the way is to remember, "It's about the other person, not you."[18]

2. Become a Servant

Jesus took the form of a slave. The Greek word in Philippians 2:7, *doulos,* is often translated as "servant," but it actually means "slave." It must have shocked the Christians in Rome who knew from their own experience what slavery looked like to find Paul introducing himself to them as "a slave of Christ Jesus" (Romans 1:1). Jesus used the same word when he said, "Whoever wants to be great among you will be your servant. Whoever wants to be first among you will be your slave—just as the [Son of Man] didn't come to be served but rather to serve and to give his life to liberate many people" (Matthew 20:26-28).

Being a servant means that we are not in charge here. We enter into the lives of others as servants who know that their lives are under the undisputed authority and control of their Lord. The Greek word for Lord is *kurios,* and it refers to one who has ownership or absolute control. The good news is that the one who has ownership or control of our lives is none other than Jesus, the one who gave the ultimate example of servanthood when he washed his disciples' feet. We go into the world as servants, not to meet our own needs—including the need to be needed—but to get in touch with the real needs of those we serve. Trevor Hudson described this attitude as "letting go of our constant preoccupations, immersing ourselves in the here and now, and giving ourselves wholeheartedly to whatever is at hand."[19]

Fans of the PBS series *Downton Abby* spent six seasons in the company of maids, butlers, and footmen who were "in service" in an English country home in the early years of the twentieth century. Carson, the butler, was the center of life for the servants "downstairs." He genuinely considered it a privilege to serve Lord Grantham. Being a servant meant that he was always on call to do whatever was necessary to meet the needs of his master and to care for the welfare of the entire house. It was never about him but always about those he served.

My wife became a servant by joining a team of women who delivered Meals on Wheels in a government housing project and some of the most underprivileged neighborhoods of Tampa. Most of the team members were from affluent families in upwardly mobile neighborhoods, but they found their place as disciples of Jesus in becoming servants of people they otherwise would never have known.

The way these women serve points in the direction of some practical ways for you to find your way to become a servant.

- They responded to a practical, clearly defined need, namely, people who are in need of a healthy meal each day.
- They were not freelancers, but served with a responsible, trustworthy agency.
- They shared the work as a part of a delivery team.
- They served by delivering the meal but were not attempting to meet every need or solve all the problems their clients faced.
- They served in a way that matched their availability.
- They were reliable and consistent in their commitment.
- They experienced joy in serving.

Like Jesus, we are called to become servants who offer our lives to meet the needs of others.

3. Learn Obedience

Jesus became obedient. The writer of the Letter to the Hebrews says that even though Jesus was the Son of God, "he learned obedience from what he suffered" (Hebrews 5:8). When we get ourselves out of the way and when we find a way to serve, sooner or later we will experience an inner compulsion that leads us to do what we know we must do in order to be obedient to the will and purpose of God. We learn obedience by allowing people who are the victims of injustice to become our teachers.

Chris Christenberry is a successful businessman who says he was "done with religion" when he slipped into the balcony of Hyde Park United Methodist Church. It began a journey that ignited a passion in his heart and led him to his way to serve. During my get-acquainted lunch with him, we were equally surprised when I felt led to invite him to join me on a mission team to South Africa and when he immediately accepted. Here's how he described the way it changed his life: "I saw the cruelty of extreme poverty. I watched as innocent children suffered from the plague of AIDS. I observed the fear induced by xenophobia. But despite these terrible experiences, I witnessed some great examples of Christian love. I saw the commitment of caregivers who were dedicated to making a positive difference in an untenable environment."

His experience in South Africa opened his eyes to the inequities in our own society and motivated him to find a way to make a difference. He began serving in a local ministry that provides housing, food, counseling, schooling, and a wide range of services to people who are homeless and those at risk of becoming homeless. He now serves on their board of directors and has engaged every person in his company as a volunteer with that ministry in the hope that they will experience the same kind of transformation that led him to serve.

Chris's story points to the way we learn obedience to the way of Christ by entering into the suffering of others. It led him to find his own way to make a difference in his own community. He experienced the movement Trevor Hudson described as the essential elements in the "Pilgrimage of Pain and Hope": encounter, reflection, and transformation that leads to obedient action.[20]

- *Encounter.* You have probably noticed a common strain in many of the stories in this book. Transformation happens most often through personal experience in which we come face-to-face with other people in their times of struggle, injustice, or pain. The challenges they face are no longer issues to be discussed but real, human needs that call for our response. Chris's encounter with both sufferers and caregivers made a transformative difference in his life.

- *Reflection.* The encounter invites us to think deeply about what we have experienced and how we will respond. We can begin to see what we encountered through the lens of deep reflection on Scripture and prayer. Without prayerful reflection, the encounter may remain as a powerful memory but never lead to obedient action. For Chris, that place of reflection was a small group of men in his congregation who, with him, were searching for the way they could make a Christlike difference in their community.

- *Transformation.* Trevor Hudson described the way "transformation…comes as a gift to those generously open to the Holy Spirit. Hearts of stone become hearts of flesh.…Compassion usually comes as a grace-soaked gift to those who intentionally, consciously, and regularly place themselves before God."[21] Chris experienced that transformation as he looked around his community and began to see the needs around him through the eyes of Christlike compassion.

- *Obedient Action.* For Chris, the only obedient response was to find a way to make a difference back home in Tampa that was consistent with the way he had seen people serve in South Africa. Encounter, reflection, and transformation led him to follow his newfound passion and find his way to make a tangible difference in the lives of people who are moving out of homelessness. He uses his business expertise in serving on the homeless ministry's board of directors and continues to participate in hands-on service with people in need. Along the way, he has expanded his impact by engaging others in that ministry.

The good news is that you do not need to go to South Africa to experience the kind of personal transformation that Chris experienced. It can happen in your own community and through your own relationships as you follow the pattern of encounter, reflection, and transformation that leads to obedient action.

The hymn or affirmation Paul imbedded in his Letter to the Philippians was an act of praise that declared the unique identity of Jesus Christ. But Paul placed it there as a challenge for each of us to "adopt the attitude that was in Christ Jesus" (Philippians 2:5). The words not only affirm who Jesus was but define who we are called to be as his followers and how we are called to serve.

My warning is that if you want your life to make a Christ-shaped difference in this world, it will mean following Jesus into places you might otherwise avoid. You may find yourself in places of pain, suffering, and injustice where words don't work. But the promise is that if you listen deeply, you will hear Christ's word of hope. It's the word that works when all other words fail.

Table Talk

Welcome to the table! Whether you join us alone or in a small group, we invite you to use these words from our panel—both on and off camera—as a springboard for reflection and discussion.

DJ: This chapter flies in the face of the idea that when you prosper, God loves you more. Rather, when we suffer we become more like Christ. My relationship with Jesus causes me to move out of my comfort zone.

LISA: We're called to people who have been cast out, condemned, and excluded; to weep with people who weep, share in suffering with people who suffer, and struggle alongside people who struggle. If we don't, we're buying into the myth that being comfortable is what God wants for us.

NICK: My journey to the faith was centered around what Christians say about suffering. At the heart of the faith is a God who suffers at the cross. We experience the presence of God in a beautiful way in the midst of all that is ugly and terrible as it is. God is so there!

LINDSEY: When we are stretched, we have new openings for God to enter into our lives. Entering places of pain is like that. It can deepen parts of us we didn't know could be deepened.

JIM: We're not idealizing suffering because suffering can be destructive. It's what we allow God to do with it that can make us strong at those broken places.

DJ: A helicopter fighter pilot is training to be a military chaplain. She said, "Pastor, you can't do the ministry I can

do because you've never experienced what we experience." She has a gift that few of us know.

NICK: The call is to intentionally enter into someone else's suffering like Jesus' call to carry our cross. It's an essential part of Christ's calling in our life.

LISA: Sometimes life is hard and takes the breath out of me—moments when I hope someone will come and be with me. In order to go to the places of suffering, we have to get up close with our own vulnerability and recognize what we need. God sends other people to be with me in my suffering. That's what we want to do for others.

JIM: To be the agent of God's hope for others we need to deal with our own unresolved stuff. If we never find healing for it, we end up projecting it on everybody else.

DJ: Suffering invites me to the mystery of God without knowing the end the story. There's something really beautiful about being a follower of Jesus and not knowing all of it. It gives me hope.

LISA: It's difficult to go to places of suffering because they highlight our humanness. Suffering makes us realize, "I'm not in control. I cannot make this thing go away." But God says, "Just go on my behalf," and God fills in the gaps.

It's your turn. How will you join the conversation?

Questions for Reflection

- When have you felt the kind of pain that Jeremiah's words describe (Jeremiah 31:2-4, 17)? Where have you seen signs of hope?
- Read Romans 8:18-38. What are your reflections on Paul's words?
- Spend some time in quiet reflection on Philippians 1:1-11. What words or phrases capture your attention?
- Which of the individual stories in this chapter speaks most deeply to you?
- What will it mean for you to empty yourself, become a servant, and learn obedience?
- How have you seen the movement from encounter, to reflection, to transformation, and finally to obedient action in your own life or the life of someone you know?

Prayer

Thou who art over us,
Thou who art one of us,
Thou who art—
Also within us,
May all see Thee—in me also....
May I also not forget the needs of others,
Keep me in Thy love
As Thou wouldest that all should be kept in mine....
Give me a pure heart—that I may see Thee,
A humble heart—that I may hear Thee,

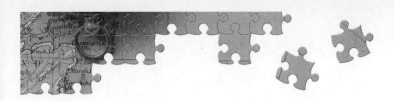

A heart of love—that I may serve Thee,
A heart of faith—that I may abide in Thee.
—Dag Hammarskjöld (1905–61) [22]

Lord, help me to enter into places of pain, suffering, and injustice and offer
your word of hope. Amen.

Action Ideas

- Look for a way to enter into someone's pain, sharing God's healing love and offering hope.
- Practice humility by letting go of self-absorbed attitudes. Remind yourself regularly, "It's not about me."
- Go where there are brothers and sisters suffering around or near you, and immerse yourself in their pain. Plan for a one-day or multiple-day immersion experience—preferably in community with others. Listen deeply with openness to what the Spirit might teach you.
- Practice the servanthood of Christ by identifying the real needs of those around you and finding a practical way to serve them.

Chapter 6

FROM HERE TO KINGDOM COME

We join our work to Heaven's gift...
High Heaven's Kingdom come on earth.
—Wendell Berry[1]

As we move toward the end of this study, let's return to Mary Oliver's question with which we began: "Tell me, what is it you plan to do with your one wild and precious life?"[2] In the end, we only have one life to live. The choices we make about what we do, how we live, where we serve, and the way we invest our energies really make a difference in our lives and become the way God uses us to make a Kingdom-shaped difference in this world.

Begin with the End

Stephen Covey taught us to "Begin with the end in mind." He sounded like an Old Testament prophet when he defined imagination as "the ability to envision in your mind what you cannot at present see with your eyes." He challenges us to "begin each day, task, or project with a clear vision of your desired direction and destination, and then continue by flexing your proactive muscles to make things happen."[3]

You may have already discovered that finding the way your one, wild, precious life can make a difference is like putting together a jigsaw puzzle. In order to find out where your piece fits in, you need to see what the final picture will ultimately be. As followers of Christ, beginning with the end in mind means grasping a biblical vision of the end or goal toward which our discipleship is leading. If our mission is making disciples who participate in God's transformation of the world, we need to capture a glimpse of what the world will look like when God's work of transformation is accomplished. It means living now in ways that are consistent with the way this world will be when God's kingdom actually comes and God's will is fully done on earth as it is in heaven.

Biblical scholars use the word *eschatology* to name the way our spiritual imagination envisions the end or goal toward which God is moving in human history. It's the ultimate fulfillment of the hope of the Old Testament prophets; the promise of the kingdom of God revealed in Jesus. It's about what this world will look like when "the kingdom of the world has become the kingdom of our Lord and his Christ" (Revelation 11:15).

One popular understanding of eschatology assumes that the goal of salvation is to get us out of this world and into the next one. This world is on a one-way, downhill roller-coaster toward destruction and our task is to prepare to leave it behind and get on to heaven. I understand the appeal of that perspective, but I don't find it to be a hopeful vision of the future. Nor does it provide guidance for our mission of making disciples "for the transformation of the world" or energize our passion to make a difference in the poverty, racism, global warming, economic injustice, and violence that undermine the biblical vision of God's intention for our world.

A more hopeful—and I would argue more biblically faithful—understanding is that God's goal is not this earth's destruction but its redemption. The end toward which we are moving is not for individual souls to be saved from this creation, but for all of us to be saved along with it. The gospel is not the story of how God gets us out of this world, but of how God came into it and how the Holy Spirit continues to be at work within it.

When John imagined the end toward which all things are moving, he saw "the holy city, New Jerusalem, *coming down* out of heaven from God." He heard a loud voice saying, "Look! God's dwelling is *here with humankind*" (Revelation 21:2-3, emphasis added). It's the picture of God's salvation in this world, not somewhere beyond it. Roman Catholic theologian Hans Küng summarized this understanding when he wrote, "God's kingdom is creation healed."[4] United Methodist bishop William H. Willimon describes the church as "the community that lives ahead of time, the people who say now what may one day be said by all, once God gets what God wants—'Your kingdom come. Your will be done, on earth as it is in heaven.'"[5]

And here's the difference-making surprise! God is inviting us to get in on the action. Eugene Peterson declares, "We are not spectators to a grand cosmic show. We are *in* the show. But we are not running it."[6] The coming of God's kingdom is only and always God's work, but we can live *now* in ways that are consistent with the way things will be *then*. By the power of the Holy Spirit, even small, apparently insignificant things can make an eternal difference.

That's what Martin Luther King Jr. was talking about the night before he died in Memphis. He told his followers that he had been to the mountain and seen the other side. He acknowledged that he might not live to get there, but it was enough to have seen the vision and played his part of its coming.

Live the Future in the Present

Archbishop Desmond Tutu affirmed this vision when he spoke to the World Methodist Conference in Nairobi, Kenya, in 1986, during some of the worst years of the struggle against apartheid in South Africa.

> Praise be to God that our God is a God of righteousness. Our God is a God of compassion. Our God is a God of liberation....God is a God who enlists us, all of us, to be fellow workers with him, to extend his kingdom of righteousness, to help change the ugliness of this world— its hatred, its enmity, its poverty, its disease, its alienation, its anxiety. He enlists us to be fellow workers with him, to transfigure it into the laughter and the joy, the compassion and the goodness, the love and the peace, the justice and the reconciliation of his kingdom as we work with him to make the kingdoms of this world to become the kingdom of our God and of his Christ.[7]

When news headlines gave little earthly evidence to support his hope, he declared the audacity of the biblical vision:

> And hey, victory is assured—victory is assured! Because the death and resurrection of our Savior Jesus Christ declares forever and ever that light has overcome darkness, that life has overcome death, that joy and laughter and peace and compassion and justice and caring and sharing...have overcome their counterparts....Praise...be to our God forever and ever.[8]

That's biblical hope! That's the hope that can sustain us when everything is stacked against it. It is hope that is grounded in the absolute faithfulness of God who will one day bring to completion the work of saving grace that became flesh in Jesus Christ (Philippians 1:6).

You may be asking, "So, what does this eschatological tour de force have to do with me?" The answer is, "Everything!" Because the end toward which we are going determines the means by which we get there. What we hope to become is what we are now becoming. What we imagine for the future shapes the way we live right now. In one of his best-loved hymns, Charles Wesley called us to "anticipate your heaven below."[10] To anticipate heaven is to live now in ways that bear witness to the way we believe the world will be when God's saving work is completed and God's redemption is accomplished. Disciples who serve most passionately in the present are people who have a firm grasp of God's future. The way they serve "now" is defined by the way they envision the world will be "then." They live in the reality of Paul's use of the words *now* and *then* in his First Letter to the Corinthians: "For *now* we see in a mirror, dimly, but *then* we will see face to face. *Now* I know only in part; *then* I will know fully, even as I have been fully known" (1 Corinthians 13:12 NRSV, emphasis added).

- We care about the environment Now because Then the renewed creation will be the place where God will be at home with God's people (Revelation 21:3).
- We work for peace Now because we know that Then swords will be turned into plowshares and spears into pruning hooks and people will not learn war anymore (Isaiah 2:4 NRSV).
- We work to overcome racism and ethnic conflict Now because we know that Then heaven will be filled with people from every race, tongue and nation (Revelation 7:9).
- We invite others to become disciples of Jesus Christ Now because we know that Then every knee will bow and every tongue confess that Jesus Christ is Lord (Philippians 2:10-11 NRSV).

- We care for one another in Christian community Now because we know that Then God will wipe away every tear from our eyes (Revelation 21:4).
- We feed the hungry, heal the sick, clothe the naked, visit the prisoners, and seek economic justice for the poor Now because Jesus said that's the way every nation will be judged Then (Matthew 25:31-46).[11]

From the earliest days of the Methodist movement, when members of the Holy Club went to serve in the prisons and orphanages of Oxford through the struggles for women's vote, child labor laws, civil rights, and movements for peace, the spirit of the Wesleys has energized Methodist disciples to find their way to make a difference in the social, political, and economic structures of their nations and communities.

Continuing in that tradition, *The Social Principles*[12] are the United Methodist expression of what it looks like to live now in ways that anticipate God's future. They are the attempt of the delegates to General Conference to respond to the critical issues of our contemporary world from a Wesleyan perspective and to guide United Methodist disciples in making a tangible difference in the complex challenges of our time.

William Reese Smith Jr. was an outstanding lawyer. When he died at the age of eighty-eight, he was celebrated as a Rhodes Scholar, the former president of the International, American, and Florida Bar associations, Distinguished Professional Lecturer of Stetson College of Law, and interim president of the University of South Florida. He had argued cases in every level of the state and federal court systems, including the Supreme Court of the United States.

Reese Smith was also a faithful United Methodist disciple who demonstrated his commitment to the Wesleyan tradition of social justice. He did everything he could to ensure that the legal system worked as well for people on the bottom rungs of society as it did for those at the top. He advocated for legal aid services for the poor and founded Florida Legal Services and the American Bar Association Center for Pro Bono Legal Services. While serving as city attorney for the city of Tampa, he played a critical role in resolving racial tensions and improving race relations. He opened the way for women and African American lawyers to emerge as leaders in his firm and in the legal community. He gave leadership to the board of trustees of Bethune-Cookman University, the State of Florida Human Rights Advocacy Committee, and the Governor's Commission on Protection and Advocacy for Persons with Developmental Disabilities. He sought and found the way his one wild and precious life could make a Kingdom-shaped difference in both his church and his community.

Most of us will not have the opportunity to impact the world the way Reese Smith did, but each of us has our own responsibility to consider how we will live in ways that anticipate God's future. You may begin by asking yourself these questions or exploring your response with your small group.

- What is my vision of the end toward which my discipleship is leading me?
- Where have I seen tangible signs of God's kingdom coming on earth as it is in heaven?
- In light of the list above, where can I make a difference *now* that is an anticipation of the way things will be *then?*

Your response to the questions may help you find your own way of living faithfully in the present in ways that anticipate God's future.

Be Faithful *Now*

Toward the end of his ministry, Jesus probed the rhetorical question, "Who then are the faithful and wise servants?" He answered the question by describing "those servants whom the master finds fulfilling their responsibilities when he comes" (Matthew 24:45-46). The image of the text was captured in an African American spiritual that says the singer will be found hoeing cotton when the Lord comes. During the final appearance of the risen Christ to the disciples before the Ascension, they asked, "Lord, are you going to restore the kingdom to Israel now?" Jesus answered, "It isn't for you to know the times or seasons that the Father has set by his own authority. Rather, you will receive power when the Holy Spirit has come upon you, and you will be my witnesses in Jerusalem, in all Judea and Samaria, and to the end of the earth" (Acts 1:6-8).

The question for us as faithful disciples is not "When is Jesus coming again?" but "What will I be doing when he gets here?" The question is not "When will Jesus' vision of the Kingdom of God be fulfilled?" but "How am I participating in that Kingdom among us right now?" Each of us can find ways to be faithful servants, participating in the Kingdom among us now.

It is becoming clearer every day that the most urgent problem besetting our Church is this: How can we live the Christian life in the modern world?
—Dietrich Bonhoeffer[13]

In 2016, I witnessed a faithful disciple participating in the Kingdom coming among us when I visited Columbus, Ohio, the day after eleven people were injured when a Somali-born Ohio State University student crashed his vehicle into pedestrians on the campus, jumped out, and began slashing others with a butcher knife before he was fatally shot by a police officer. When Bishop Gregory Palmer met me at the airport, he told me that we had been invited to a gathering of United

Methodists and leaders from the Islamic community that evening. I listened deeply as the imam described the way he was caring for the family of the young man who had been shot. A Muslim woman who leads an outreach program with young adults wept as she wondered if they might have been able to help this young man and thereby prevent this tragedy.

Toward the end of the evening, a United Methodist woman said that a few weeks prior, she had felt a leading by the Holy Spirit to get acquainted with some members of the Islamic community. Obeying that prompting by the Spirit, she called the local mosque and was given the name of a family who might be interested. She invited that family to her home for supper. The invitation was returned and she went to dinner in their home. Her congregation was already planning a Methodist-Muslim potluck supper in the near future. She sensed that the Spirit of God had begun this work in her life in preparation for the crisis the community was facing. It was a joyful witness to the difference one person can make toward healing the brokenness of our world; a living expression of the kingdom of God alive among us pointing toward God's ultimate healing of the whole human family.

Make a Big Difference in Little Things

Confronted by the sheer magnitude of the challenges we face, it would be easy to begin to think that the little things we do don't really make a difference. Perhaps Jesus anticipated that possibility when he gave us his parable of the mustard seed (Matthew 13:31-32; Mark 4: 30-32; Luke 13:18-19) as a word of encouragement. Digging into the way the Gospel writers retell that parable, biblical scholar Amy-Jill Levine pointed to four ways in which the parable can guide us in our service.

- "No seed is, or should be, seen as insignificant; each contains life within it.... Even small actions, or hidden actions, have the potential to produce great things."[14]

In a world that is intoxicated with bigness, we can easily be tempted to think that the little things we do make no difference. But in God's economy, everything matters and every action either contributes to, or gets in the way of, God's kingdom becoming a reality in human history. What you do with your one, wild and precious life really makes a difference!

- "Some things need to be *left alone*.... Not everything, or even everyone, needs our constant attention."[15]

Just because we are doing God's work doesn't mean that we have to be doing it all the time. God built Sabbath into the creation so that we can learn the rhythm of work and rest, labor and leisure. I've known too many well-intended people who burned themselves out because they did not learn this lesson. As a hyperactive, type A extrovert who is genetically infected by Germanic seriousness, I learned an important lesson from a baseball player friend who said, "Jim, you don't have to swing at every pitch."

- "Sometimes we need to *get out of the way*.... Who sowed it is much less important than the tree into which the seed grows."[16]

We make a Kingdom-shaped difference when we invest our energy, time, and talents in a vision larger than our own self-interest. The mission is always more important than we are. Instead of drawing attention to ourselves, we serve with genuine humility that enables us to support, encourage, and celebrate God's work wherever it happens and whoever is doing it. We are more likely to use the pronouns "we" and "our" than "I" and "mine." Our passion is not to build up our own image, but to build the team with whom we serve.

- "The kingdom of heaven is found in what today we might call 'our own backyard.'"[17]

We don't necessarily need to be looking off to some distant horizon to find our calling. God only calls a few heroic souls to go to distant places. Most of God's work in this world gets done in ordinary places by ordinary people like us who see our world through the extraordinary perspective of God's Kingdom revealed in Jesus Christ. The task to which God calls us is often the task most closely at hand. At the same time, we remain open to the possibility that God may enlarge our vision and call us to make a difference in ways and means that stretch out beyond our immediate boundaries. God has a surprising way of expanding our small efforts to touch the world in ways that go beyond anything we expected.

Engage the Systems

Making a difference that bears witness to the reign and rule of God among us can also lead us to serve as a representative of God's kingdom in the political, legal, and economic structures and systems of our community, nation, and world.

Tally Wells is one of those faithful servants who followed his passion and found his calling and his place to serve through advocacy. His journey began when he was growing up in a home that was deeply rooted in the faith and passionately committed to make a difference in the world. He also points to a vibrant local church that challenged him to take the road less traveled. He says he was "blessed with people who taught me—or better yet, showed me—what it means to follow Jesus."

At Duke University, he wrestled with whether God might be calling him to the ordained ministry. He joined his wife in serving with the L'Arche community that engages deeply in the lives of people with disabilities. Listening to Jesus' words in the Beatitudes and Matthew 25, he felt called to respond to Jesus' call to be with the poor and marginalized. As a student at Harvard School of Education and Duke Law School, it became clear that he had talent for the law that could be used on behalf of people who are often neglected. He realized that he could use his gifts "to bring people to the table who otherwise would be left out and to enable them to access the resources and justice they are often denied." Instead of following the more typical path that leads to a prestigious law firm bringing down an equally prestigious salary, he joined the Atlanta Legal Aid Society as their director of disability integration project where he leads a team of disability advocates in seeking integrated support for people with disabilities through litigation, policy work, and the news media.

When asked about the personal challenges he faces, he acknowledged that like everyone else, he is tempted by the desire to provide for his family with a job that pays a higher salary. But he is willing to make that sacrifice in order to live out his passion and is grateful for the support of his family. He finds supportive community in his friendships, the network of people of various faith traditions who are also dedicated to social justice, and his local United Methodist congregation. He experiences hope in the clients he serves who face sacrifices and challenges greater than his own, and by seeing the "transformative changes" that are the result of his work and from "seeing lived out what Jesus promised." In spite of political roadblocks and economic challenges along the way, he lives with a joyful confidence that the long arc of history always bends toward justice.

As followers of Jesus, we practice our discipleship in the context of the social, economic, and political structures and systems within which we work and live: schools, businesses, neighborhood organizations, political action groups, social organizations, religious institutions, and governments. While none of these exist primarily to represent the kingdom of God, each one provides a setting in which faithful disciples can make a difference that bears witness to our commitment to Jesus' description of that Kingdom. We may not be called to transform the entire system, but we are called to be the agents of God's healing, hope, justice, and peace within them. It's what Jesus meant when he said that his disciples would be "like yeast, which a woman took and hid in a bushel of wheat flour until the yeast had worked its way through all the dough" (Matthew 13:33).

Offer Your "Stubborn Ounces"

Whether we serve close to home or across the globe, whether we engage in simple acts of faithful service or become agents of change within the political, economic, and social systems and structures around us, each of us can do *something* to make a difference. Mother Teresa often reminded us that we are called to do small things with great love. Living with the mind of Christ often leads to what poet Bonaro Overstreet called "Stubborn Ounces." The poet, psychologist, and lifelong defender of civil liberties and academic freedom dedicated her poem "Stubborn Ounces" "To One Who Doubts the Worth of Doing Anything if You Can't Do Everything." Overstreet acknowledged that sometimes the little efforts we make don't seem to make much of a difference. They appear to be nothing more than small ounces dropped onto "the hovering scale where Justice hangs in balance." She went on to say that she never had any illusion that her little efforts would tip the scales of justice. She was, however, irrevocably convinced of her "right to choose which side/shall feel the stubborn ounces of my weight."[18]

I discovered—or was given—Overstreet's poem shortly before my first visit to South Africa. Confronted with the massive problems of racism and poverty that are the ongoing inheritance of apartheid, it would have been easy to start thinking that there is no way one person could make a difference. But as I saw people caring for HIV/ AIDS patients at Hillcrest AIDS Center, teaching children in township preschools, providing meals for day laborers, and pouring their energy into building the economic and social structures of a new nation, I returned many times to Overstreet's words. It has, in fact, become an essential part of the way I live out my obedience to Jesus Christ. Each of us might think our efforts are insignificant, but they are the witness of our desire to choose which side in the scales of good and evil will feel the stubborn ounces of our weight.

Being obedient to the love of Christ at work in this world often means offering small things, our "stubborn ounces," in the absolute trust in the God who promises to use whatever we have to give in ways that fulfill God's purpose in this world. The boy who offered Jesus his five barley loaves and two small fish never could have anticipated the way his gifts would be multiplied to meet the needs of thousands (John 6:8-15). We may not see or know the end result, but it will have been enough to know that we used the gifts we were given to make a difference along the way.

I'm reminded of a woman in our congregation who had a vision of a teddy bear ministry in which small bears would be scattered around the pews of the church, each one with a note attached saying that it represented the prayers and concern of our congregation. She believed that the Spirit would guide people who needed that encouragement to sit by one of the bears when they came to worship. I underestimated the importance of her ministry, but I was wrong. She was faithfully following her passion and had found her way to serve. Almost every Sunday, people would come to me after worship with tears in their eyes and one of those bears in their hands. They would tell me about the family member or friend to whom they would deliver it and ask me to pray with them. When I visited in hospitals and nursing homes, I was often welcomed by one of those bears sitting beside the patient or find someone holding a bear in their arms as a sign of God's love for them. In a few years' time, more than one thousand bears had gone from the sanctuary as a witness of the church's love and concern. It was a small act of kindness that made a big difference in the lives of both the persons who gave and the persons who received them. Those little bears became a finite expression of the infinite compassion of God.

There remains for us only the very narrow way...of living every day as if it were our last, and yet living in faith and responsibility as though there were to be a great future....It may be that the day of judgment will dawn tomorrow; and in that case, though not before, we shall gladly stop working for a better future.
—Dietrich Bonhoeffer[19]

Be Faithful to the End

In the end, our calling is not to be successful, but to be obedient. The painful reality is that when we confront the kingdoms of this earth with the vision of the kingdom of God, there is no guarantee that we will see every wrong made right, every injustice corrected, or every broken life made whole. When we stand up as peacemakers in a world that is addicted to violence, for equality in a culture that is infected with racism, for powerless, marginalized people in a world controlled by the powerful, or for "freedom and justice for all" in a culture of fear and oppression, there is no promise that we will immediately see the results of our actions. But we serve in the assurance that there will be a day when every broken heart is healed, every injustice has been made right, every tear is dried, and the whole creation will rejoice.

That was the confidence in which John Wesley wrote his last letter to William Wilberforce, who was leading the movement against slavery in Parliament. From his deathbed, Wesley offered these words of encouragement:

> Unless God has raised you up for this very thing, you will be worn out by the opposition of men and devils. But if God before you, who can be against you? Are all of them together stronger than God? O be not weary of well doing! Go on, in the name of God and in the power of his might, till even American slavery (the vilest that ever saw the sun) shall vanish away before it.[20]

In our attempts to make a difference, we all need the kind of encouragement, support, and prayer that Wesley provided for Wilberforce. A couple with whom I have shared four decades of friendship found that kind of encouragement in a Christian community in Washington, D.C., during the years of the civil rights movement and opposition to the war in Vietnam. For their wedding vows, they made their own adaptation of the benediction with which the members of their community were sent from their worship into the world.

As they remember it, the prayer acknowledged that their call to discipleship would sometimes set them in accord with and sometimes in opposition to the structures of the society around them. As they prepared to face their tasks each week, they prayed that they would pour their whole lives into their mission without regard to opposition, inner weariness, or condemnation. They prayed for tenaciousness to hold onto their vision until the final battle is over, and for nonchalance in knowing that the final outcome will not depend on their efforts. They committed themselves to act with power as if everything depended on them, but with detachment because they knew that nothing they did would last forever. Across the years, that prayer has guided them to find their one wild and precious way to make a difference.

Paul encouraged the Galatian disciples with these words: "Let's not get tired of doing good, because in time we'll have a harvest if we don't give up" (Galatians 6:9). An old African American spiritual put the words to music:

> Walk together children, don't you get weary,
> walk together children, don't you get weary,
> walk together children, don't you get weary,
> there's a great camp meeting in the promised land.[21]

May each of us do what we can with our one wild and precious life to make a difference in the assurance that one day God's redeeming purpose for this world will be accomplished and we will have the great joy of knowing that by following our passion and finding our place to serve, we were a part of its coming. Thanks be to God!

Table Talk

Welcome to the table! Whether you join us alone or in a small group, we invite you to use these words from our panel—both on and off camera—as a springboard for reflection and discussion.

JIM: We're always on an upward journey toward the fulfillment of God's kingdom. What does that Kingdom look like to you?

LISA: The Kingdom is already unfolding by how we choose to live. Martin Luther King Jr. said the arc of the moral universe bends toward justice. But it bends because we're willing it to bend it with every fiber of our being.

NICK: Scripture speaks of the great reversal—the high brought down, the low lifted up. It's the picture of everybody flourishing, having enough.

LISA: Because Christ overcame the grave and all things have been made new, I believe that one morning not one child…is going to be hungry; that I won't see a prostitute on the street because no one has to sell her body to have what she needs; a world where there are more folks walking on trails and going to school than there are behind prison bars. Will we live like we believe it?

DJ: A woman said, "I'm willing. I just don't know what God's calling me to do." Later, a younger woman with her three-year-old daughter needed someone to give her space to care for her daughter so she wouldn't have to do what she'd been doing to survive. This week, those women are moving in together. It was grace unfolding.

NICK: Being with you here today and listening to what you're doing tells me there are a lot more mustard seeds than we think there are. If all we do is listen to how bad things are, we come to believe that the world is an awful place while there are phenomenal things happening all around. God often surprises us by opening some door that we never noticed.

LINDSEY: The mustard seed is small, but the bush it produces is big. I've seen the fruit mustard seeds produce—people mobilizing on prison reform, standing up for affordable health care and housing, calling their legislators. I've seen bad laws come down and better ones put in their place. They are seeds of movements that can transform our whole system.

NICK: One of the lies we buy into is that…what we do doesn't matter. But people who make the biggest difference realize, "I have something to offer!"

LINDSEY: We have one life and it is up to us how we use it. We can do something, or we can think we don't have anything to offer. My hope is that people will do something whether it seems small or has larger ripples.

JIM: God told Moses, "Get going!" Whatever the next step is, take that step and see where God leads you.

So, it's your turn, not just to join the conversation but to make a difference!

Questions for Reflection

- How do you imagine the end toward which all things are moving?
- Where have you seen signs of the kingdom of God coming among us in specific acts of compassion, justice, reconciliation, or peace?
- What sustains your hope for the future?
- How do you see yourself engaging with the social, economic, and political systems of our world?
- What are your next steps as you follow your passion and find your place to serve?

Prayer

Holy Spirit of God, who at Pentecost descended with power upon Christ's disciples…make us more than ourselves, because we have you for our ally and reinforcement….Save us from our timidities and fears, from the reluctance and paralysis of our uncertainties and doubt. Nerve us…that we may be strong to endure, to sacrifice, and to achieve. Since you have called us into an unfinished world to bear a hand with you in its completion, give us wisdom and strength that we may work while it is day, ere the night comes, when no one can work. Amen.
—*Harry Emerson Fosdick (1878–1969)*[22]

Lord, may your Kingdom become a reality here and now as I do what I can to make a difference in this world. Amen.

Action Ideas

- Write a description of your vision of God's future. Choose each day to live Now in ways that are consistent with the ways things will be Then.
- Look for something you can do each day to help God's kingdom come on earth as it is in heaven.
- Take time to celebrate God's work wherever you see it happening and whoever may be doing it. Pray for and encourage those who are doing God's kingdom work.
- Be intentional about building up those who are serving with or alongside you.
- Remember that the task to which God calls us is often the task most closely at hand. Identify what that task is today and pursue it.
- Make a list of small things that have yielded big results—whether they are your acts or those of others. Keep the list and add to it as God continues to work in and through you and those around you.
- Explore ways you might serve in the political, legal, and economic structures and systems in which you live and work (schools, businesses, political action groups, religious institutions, neighborhood organizations, governments).

NOTES

Introduction

1. Mary Oliver, "The Summer Day," in *New and Selected Poems* (Boston, Mass.: Beacon, 1992), 94.

2. From *The Book of Discipline of The United Methodist Church*, 2016 (Nashville: The United Methodist Publishing House, 2016), ¶120. Used by permission.

3. Richard Rohr, *Falling Upward* (San Francisco: Jossey-Bass, 2011), 110.

4. See *A Disciple's Path: Deepening Your Relationship with Christ and the Church* (Nashville: Abingdon, 2012); and *A Disciple's Heart: Growing in Love and Grace* (Nashville: Abingdon, 2015) for in-depth explorations of the essential practices of discipleship formation.

Chapter 1

1. Annie Dillard, *An American Childhood* (New York: Harper & Row, 1987), 248.

2. Dag Hammarskjöld, *Markings* (New York: Knopf, 1966), 205.

3. Friedrich Nietzsche, *Beyond God and Evil*, https://www.marxists.org/reference/archive/nietzsche/1886/beyond-good-evil/ch05.htm.

4. That story is told in *You Only Have to Die: Leading Your Congregation to New Life* (Nashville: Abingdon, 2004).

5. From "The Present Crisis" (December 1844) found in *The Complete Poetical Works of James Russell Lowell, 1848*; also found in "Once to Every Man and Nation," https://www.poets.org/poetsorg/poem/present-crisis.

6. Richard Rohr, *Falling Upward* (San Francisco: Jossey-Bass, 2011), ix.

7. *The United Methodist Hymnal* (Nashville: Abingdon, 1989), 37.

8. Evelyn Underhill, *Selections from the Writings of Evelyn Underhill*, quoted in *A Guide to Prayer for All Who Walk with God* (Nashville: Upper Room Books, 2013), 180.

9. Diana L. Hynson, "Teachers Understand the United Methodist Church," https://www.umcdiscipleship.org/resources/teachers-understand-the-united-methodist-church.

10. Washington Irving, "Rip Van Winkle, a Posthumous Writing of Diedrich Knickerbocker," http://www.bartleby.com/310/2/1.html.

11. Elizabeth Barrett Browning, "From 'Aurora Leigh,'" http://www.bartleby.com/236/86.html.

12. Doris Kerns Goodwin, *The Bully Pulpit* (New York: Simon & Schuster, 2013), 250.

13. Tony Millett, "The Fiftieth Anniversary of Churchill's Funeral Brings Many Memories for Trumpeter Basil King," *Marlborough News*, February 3, 2015, http://www.marlboroughnewsonline.co.uk/features/general/3886-the-fiftieth-anniversary-of-churchill-s-funeral-brings-many-memories-for-trumpeter-basil-king.

14. Steve Garnaas-Holmes, "Stay awake," Unfolding Light, https://www.unfoldinglight.net/archive.

Chapter 2

1. "Albert Schweitzer's Leadership for Life," http://aschweitzer.com/abouta.html.

2. Jeffrey Kluger, "The Happiness of Pursuit," July 8, 2013, http://content.time.com/time/magazine/article/0,9171,2146449,00.html.

3. Harry Emerson Fosdick, "God of Grace and God of Glory," *The United Methodist Hymnal* (Nashville: Abingdon, 1989), 577.

4. David Brooks, *The Road to Character* (New York: Random House, 2015), xvi.

5. Becca Stevens, *Snake Oil: The Art of Healing and Truth-Telling* (New York: Jericho, 2013), 164–65.

6. Richard Rohr, *Falling Upward* (San Francisco: Jossey-Bass), ix.

7. Eduardo J. Lango, "I'll Be Listening," http://www.hymnary.org/text/when_he_calls_me_i_will_answer.

8. E. Stanley Jones, *Selections from E. Stanley Jones*, comp. Eunice Jones Mathews and James K. Mathews (Nashville: Abingdon, 1972), 132–33.

9. Geffrey B. Kelly and F. Burton Nelson, eds., *The Cost of Moral Leadership* (Grand Rapids: Eerdmans, 2003), 226.

10. Rueben P. Job, *A Wesleyan Spiritual Reader* (Nashville: Abingdon, 1997), 15.

11. John Wesley, *The Works of John Wesley*, ed. Thomas Jackson (Grand Rapids: Zondervan), 1:99.

12. John Wesley, *The Works of John Wesley*, ed. Thomas Jackson (Grand Rapids: Zondervan), 3:213.

13. John Wesley, *The Works of John Wesley*, ed. Ted A. Campbell (Nashville: Abingdon, 2015), 3:204.

14. James A Harnish, *A Disciple's Heart* (Nashville: Abingdon, 2015), 119–121.

15. Albert Schweitzer, *Out of My Life and Thought* (New York: Henry Holt, 1990), 82.

16. Frances R. Havergal, "Master, speak! They servant heareth," http://www
.hymnary.org/text/master_speak_thy_servant_heareth, public domain.

Chapter 3

1. Frederick Buechner, *Wishful Thinking: A Theological ABC* (New York: Harper & Row, 1973), 95.

2. Joel Kilpatrick, "Woman Embalmed, Bronzed in Favorite Pew," http://www
.larknews.com/archives/301.

3. Dietrich Bonhoeffer, *No Rusty Swords* (New York: Harper & Row, 1965), 154.

4. *The Book of Discipline of the United Methodist Church, 2016* (Nashville: The United Methodist Publishing House, 2016), ¶122, http://www.umc.org/what
-we-believe/section-1-the-churches.

5. Author's paraphrase of Mark 16:7.

6. Charles Wesley, "Maker in Whom We Live," *The United Methodist Hymnal* (Nashville: Abingdon, 1989), 88.

7. Dietrich Bonhoeffer, *The Cost of Discipleship*, trans. R. H. Fuller (New York: Macmillan, 1948), 49.

8. Peter Marshall, *Mr. Jones Meet the Master* (New York: Fleming H. Revell, 1950), 49, 57.

9. John Ortberg, *The Life You've Always Wanted* (Grand Rapids: Zondervan, 1997), 81.

10. David Brooks, *The Road to Character* (New York: Random House, 2015), 20.

11. Ibid., 46.

12. *Holy Women, Holy Men: Celebrating the Saints* (New York: Church Publishing, 2010), 369.

13. Chad Smith, "Local Clergy Come Together to Respond to Dove World," *The Gainesville Sun*, August 25, 2010, http://www.gainesville.com/news/20100825
/local-clergy-come-together-to-respond-to-dove-world.

Chapter 4

1. Act 1, Scene 5.

2. Ibid.

3. Rinker Buck, *The Oregon Trail* (New York: Simon & Schuster, 2015), 162.

4. Becca Stevens, *Letters from the Farm: A Simple Path for a Deeper Spiritual Life* (New York; Morehouse, 2015), 39–41.

5. Dietrich Bonhoeffer, *Life Together* (San Francisco: HarperSanFrancisco, 1954), 19–20.

6. Bernard Mayo, ed., *Jefferson Himself* (Charlottesville: University Press of Virginia, 1942), 295–96.

7. John Wesley, *Catholic Spirit*, http://www.umcmission.org/Find-Resources /John-Wesley-Sermons/Sermon-39-Catholic-Spirit.

8. Eugene Peterson, *Christ Plays in Ten Thousand Places* (Grand Rapids: Eerdmans, 2005), 203.

9. John Wesley, "The Duty of Constant Communion," http://www.umcmission .org/Find-Resources/John-Wesley-Sermons/Sermon-101-The-Duty-of -Constant-Communion.

10. "A Service of Word and Table I and Introductions to the Other Forms," *The United Methodist Hymnal* (Nashville: Abingdon, 1989), 10–11, emphasis added.

11. John Winthrop, "A Model of Christian Charity," http://winthropsociety.com /doc_charity.php.

12. Stevens, *Letters from the Farm*, 96–97.

13. Charles Wesley, "All Praise to Our Redeeming Lord," *The United Methodist Hymnal* (Nashville; Abingdon, 1989), 554.

Chapter 5

1. Peter Storey, *With God in the Crucible* (Nashville: Abingdon, 2002), 80–81.

2. Act 5, scene 3.

3. J. B. Phillips, *The New Testament in Modern English* (London: Geoffrey Bles, 1960), 328.

4. Rueben P. Job, Norman Shawchuck, John S. Mogabgab, *A Guide to Prayer for All Who Walk with God* (Nashville: Upper Room , 2013), 245.

5. Geoffrey Rowell, ed., *The English Religious Tradition and the Genius of Anglicanism* (Nashville: Abingdon, 1992), 53.

6. Geffrey B. Kelly and F. Burton Nelson, *The Cost of Moral Leadership* (Grand Rapids: Eerdmans, 2003), 173–75.

7. Job, Shawchuck, Mogabgab, *A Guide to Prayer*, 245.

8. Ibid., 129–30.

9. Richard Rohr, *Falling Upward* (San Francisco: Jossey-Bass, 2011), 122.

10. Tom McCloskey, interviewed by Dave Begnaud, *CBS Evening News*, June 19, 2016.

11. David Brooks, *The Road to Character* (New York: Random House, 2015), 93–95.

12. Becca Stevens, *Snake Oil: The Art of Healing and Truth-Telling* (New York: Jericho, 2013), 62–63.

13. Charles Wesley, "And Can It Be that I Should Gain," *The United Methodist Hymnal* (Nashville: Abingdon, 1989), 363.

14. George Herbert, *The Temple*, https://www.ccel.org/h/herbert/temple/Bag.html.

15. Trevor Hudson, *A Mile in My Shoes* (Nashville: Upper Room, 2005), 17.

16. Ibid., 41.

17. Ibid., 18.

18. Becca Stevens, *Letters from the Farm: A Simple Path for a Deeper Spiritual Life* (New York; Morehouse, 2015), 14.

19. Hudson, *A Mile in My Shoes*, 30.

20. Hudson, ibid., 20–24.

21. Hudson, ibid., 21–22, 24.

22. Dag Hammarskjöld, *Markings* (New York: Knopf, 1966), 100.

Chapter 6

1. Wendell Berry, *A Timbered Choir* (Berkeley: Counterpoint, 1998), 49.

2. Mary Oliver, Mary Oliver, "The Summer Day," in *New and Selected Poems* (Boston, Mass.: Beacon, 1992), 94.

3. Stephen Covey, "The 7 Habits of Highly Effective People; Habit 2: Begin with the End in Mind," https://www.stephencovey.com/7habits/7habits-habit2.php.

4. Hans Küng, *On Being a Christian*, trans. Edward Quinn (Garden City, N.Y.: Doubleday, 1976), 231.

5. William H. Willimon, *Who Will Be Saved?* (Nashville: Abingdon, 2008), 58.

6. Eugene Peterson, *Practice Resurrection* (Grand Rapids: Eerdmans, 2010), 68.

7. Joe Hale, ed., *Proceedings of the Fifteenth World Methodist Conference* (Lake Junaluska, N.C.: World Methodist Council, 1987), 168.

8. Hale, *Proceedings of the Fifteenth World Methodist Conference*, 169.

9. Charles Wesley, "Let Us Plead for Faith Alone," http://www.umcmission.org/Find-Resources/Global-Praise-/Charles-Wesley-Hymns/Let-Us-Plead-for-Faith-Alone.

10. Charles Wesley, "O For a Thousand Tongues to Sing," *The United Methodist Hymnal* (Nashville: Abingdon, 1989), 57.

11. Adapted from James A. Harnish, *A Disciple's Heart: Growing in Love and Grace* (Nashville: Abingdon, 2015), 113–114.

12. "Social Principles and Social Creed," *The Book of Resolutions of The United Methodist Church, 2016 (Nashville: United Methodist Publishing House, 2016),* www.umc.org/what-we-believe/social-principles-social-creed.

13. Dietrich Bonhoeffer, *The Cost of Discipleship*, trans. R. H. Fuller (New York: Macmillan, 1948), 49.

14. Amy-Jill Levine, *Short Stories by Jesus* (New York: HarperOne, 2014), 182.

15. Ibid.

16. Ibid.

17. Ibid.

18. Bonaro Overstreet, *Signature: New and Selected Poems* (New York: Norton, 1978), 19.

19. Dietrich Bonhoeffer, *Letters and Papers from Prison* (New York: Macmillan, 1971), 15–16.

20. "Letter to William Wilberforce," http://www.umcmission.org/Find-Resources /John-Wesley-Sermons/The-Wesleys-and-Their-Times/Letter-to-William -Wilberforce.

21. "Walk Together Children," http://www.hymnary.org/tune/walk_together _children.

22. Harry Emerson Fosdick, *A Book of Public Prayers* (New York: Harper, 1959), 140–141, adapted.